BLACKJACK:
A Champion's Guide

First published by Gaming Books, 2013
Gaming Books is an imprint of John Hunt Publishing Ltd., Laurel House, Station Approach,
Alresford, Hants, SO24 9JH, UK
office1@jhpbooks.net
www.johnhuntpublishing.com

For distributor details and how to order please visit the 'Ordering' section on our website.

Text copyright: Dario De Toffoli and Margherita Bonaldi 2013

ISBN: 978 1 78099 609 7

Printed in the USA by Edwards Brothers Malloy

We operate a distinctive and ethical publishing philosophy in all areas of
our business, from our global network of authors to production and
worldwide distribution.

DARIO DE TOFFOLI
MARGHERITA BONALDI

BLACKJACK:
A Champion's Guide

GAMING BOOKS

Winchester, UK
Washington, USA

In collaboration with:

www.studiogiochi.com

Graphic project: Rossana Nardo

Thanks to:
Cosimo Cardellicchio, Leo Colovini, Dario Zaccariotto, Jokonline.

CONTENTS

FOREWORD

Blackjack: A Champion's Guide is the definitive guide to winning in Blackjack. Blackjack is a game of odds, and this book will teach you to play the odds in your favor rather than just chasing dumb luck. It also examines how the odds and best play changes with different casino rules ranging from the States to Europe and Asia. This book is a real treat. While demystifying the strategies and mathematical probabilities behind optimal Blackjack play, authors Dario De Toffoli and Margherita Bonaldi provide enlightening anecdotes from popular culture with films including *Rain Man* and TV's *Lost*. *Blackjack: A Champion's Guide* delves into the nuances of gameplay in Blackjack, and is guaranteed to make you a better Blackjack player.

Margherita Bonaldi is a mathematician who specializes in probabilistic modeling and behavioral strategies in Blackjack. Meanwhile, **Dario De Toffoli** is one of the strongest games players in the world--winning the Pentamind World Championship twice at the Mind Sports Olympiad. De Toffoli is also the founder of Studiogiochi, a games company, and a bestselling author on games ranging from poker to backgammon.

Play the odds and enjoy the ride!
Etan Ilfeld

INTRODUCTION

There are those who interpret games of chance as pure escapism, something to get a buzz. In some ways, studying probabilities, seeking to control chance and adopting the most rational behaviour at all times detracts from their legitimate amusement. This book is not for them, reading it would only spoil their fun.

We, however, believe, just as the great Pierre Simon de Laplace taught us in his unparalleled *A Philosophical Essay on Probabilities*, that probability is a tool that can bring us closer to the objective reality, where this is too complicated to be reconstructed and anticipated in rational terms.

Two centuries have passed since the first edition of the Essay was published (1812), but the power of his thought is still not common knowledge, newspapers still print criminal features recommending lottery numbers to unwary readers and there are still people who believe the Roulette ball has a memory of its own.

Laplace warns that "we ought always in the conduct of life to make the product of the benefit hoped for, by its probability, at least equal to the similar product relative to the loss. But it is necessary, in order to attain this, to appreciate exactly the advantages, the losses and their respective probabilities. For this a great accuracy of mind, a delicate judgement, and a great experience in affairs is necessary; it is necessary to know how to guard one's self against prejudices, illusions of fear and hope, and erroneous ideas, ideas of fortune and happiness, with which the majority of people feed their self-love."

Well, it's not always easy to follow Laplace's suggestions in real life; in fact it's far too difficult to consistently make the best decisions without a general understanding of what is happening, why it is happening and what might happen. But in games of chance we can indeed get an idea of 'where we're coming from', 'what we're doing' and even 'where we might go', that is, all the final situations in which we might find ourselves, each with its very own set of probabilities.

I certainly would not want to deny the ever decisive role of Lady Luck, but awareness of your behaviour leads to statistically better results, the pleasure of using reason and, what's more, protection from compulsivity.

On Blackjack

Once upon a time, a friend of mine was playing Blackjack. And I was watching him. I noticed that on several occasions he did not follow the well-known tables that show the best way to behave in every game situation and I tactfully enquired why not. He was gobsmacked that I believed in those tables. According to him they were only distributed to condition players into playing to the dealer's favour. No, no, much better to trust your instinct!

His reasoning is easily refuted on the basis that it certainly was not the casinos that distributed the tables, but whatever makes him happy.

Nevertheless, to better counter his argument, I began to consult publications on Blackjack. Dozens of them showed these mythical tables, but not a single one took the trouble to explain them. "Sooner or later", I thought, "I'll have to calculate them myself!"

And the perfect opportunity arose a few years later, in the guise of Margherita Bonaldi, grappling with choosing a topic for a mathematics thesis on games of chance.

"Can you suggest anything?"

"Yes absolutely! The tables for the Blackjack basic strategy need to be demonstrated. They need to be recalculated whilst clearly explaining how to proceed."

"Ok, it sounds interesting."

Deal done. The professor accepted and thus the thesis *Modelli probabilistici e strategie di comportamento nel gioco del blackjack* (Probabilistic models and behaviour strategies in the game of Blackjack) was born. The language is for beginners – as strictly demanded by the academic world – but it had substance. At this point I had an idea, why not transform these preliminary calculations into an actual essay on Blackjack? There was no doubt that we had the opportunity to create an entirely new product, despite there already being a vast amount of material on the topic.

And that is precisely what we did. We analysed every game situation in detail and recalculated all the tables, explaining them every step of the way.

And don't panic, they're all correct!

But for us the recalculations themselves were a fascinating mathematical adventure, a pleasure of the intellect.

What is more, we introduced the concept of the 'mathematical hope' of every possible game situation; to borrow from Laplace, it is the "product of the sum hoped for by the probability of obtaining it".

We don't just tell you what to do, but explain – for anyone interested – why you need to do it, what your chances of victory are and how serious the setback will be if you make the wrong decision.

All of this is extensively illustrated with tables and graphics and we strived to make them as explanatory as possible. In short, you can't go wrong by consulting, rather than reading, the chapter *How to play and why,* every play is made clear and there are no longer any ifs and buts to hold you back.

Once you have absorbed the basic strategy, there is of course a chapter devoted to the advanced strategies and card-counting strategies made famous by novels and films. But don't get any strange ideas; the epic days of the card-counting teams who got rich quick are long gone. Just make do with applying the basic strategy as best you can.

Dario De Toffoli, January 2011

BLACKJACK

"I selected from my valuables such as seemed most important and useful and I did not fail to include this pack of cards among them", here the speaker exhibited that oviform specimen already mentioned, "and with these I have gained my bread among the inns and taverns between Madrid and this place, by playing at Vingt-et-un. It is true they are somewhat soiled and worn, as your worship sees; but for him who knows how to handle them, they possess a marvellous virtue, which is, that you never cut them but you find an ace at the bottom; if your worship then is acquainted with the game, you will see what an advantage it is to know for certain that you have an ace to begin with, since you may count it either for one or eleven; and so you may be pretty sure that when the stakes are laid at twenty-one, your money will be much disposed to stay at home."

Rinconete and Cortadillo (Exemplary Novels, 1613)
Miguel de Cervantes

Blackjack is one of the most interesting casino games because it involves real decision making. And what is more, the dealer's advantage can be reduced to practically nothing if you play your cards right.

So why do the casinos offer it? What do they stand to gain?

The fact is that for the most part players do not possess the skills required, all too often they tend not to make the most favourable decisions, only to bemoan the bad luck that follows them, and besides, they do not have the necessary discipline. There are charts that tell us what the best move is in every situation, but most players simply do not use them or do not trust them or perhaps do not even know of their existence. They trust their instinct over mathematics.

But Blackjack is based entirely on mathematics!

In all other casino games memory counts for nothing, what has already happened (the roll of the dice, the toss of the ball) has no influence whatsoever on what will happen next. In Blackjack however, the cards dealt in previous hands determine a variation, sometimes an appreciable variation, of probability in favour of the player. And since the player has the option of varying his bet, this allows him to bet more in situations that are to his favour and less in less-advantageous situations. This is the weapon that professionals use to gain an advantage over the casinos.

HISTORY

There is no reliable documentation of the history of Blackjack; in fact, it is the product of a series of evolutions, as is the case for most modern card games.

Its most direct ancestor is the French game of Vingt et Un (Twenty one), which has existed in France since the early seventeenth century; modern Blackjack has more or less the same structure, although the individual rules have undergone various transformations, especially in those early years. For example, the role of the dealer used to be shared among the players, who played against each other; any player who got 21 with just two cards became dealer.

Vingt et Un derives in turn from older games that had the same structure, where victory was determined by the total numerical value of the cards held by each player. Among these are the French Quinze (Fifteen), which dates back to the sixteenth century and the Italian Sette e mezzo (Seven and a Half). Even older still is the Spanish Venunia, which appeared for the first time in the fifteenth century and was mentioned by Miguel de Cervantes, author of *Don Quixote*, in his *Novelas ejemplares* (The Exemplary Novels, 1613).

The game of 21 was brought to America towards the late eighteenth century by immigrants from Europe. But in the United States of the early nineteenth century, games of chance were illegal almost everywhere.

It was in New Orleans, Louisiana, that in virtue of an 1820 law the first luxurious gaming centres began to emerge, complete with high-class restaurants and clientele.

The situation in Nevada, the present-day Mecca for gamblers, on the other hand, was quite curious. Since the early nineteenth century small illegal casinos in saloons or even mines had been widespread and were legalised in 1869. But in 1910 all house-banked games were banned and therefore 21 was played as a player-banked game until 1931, meaning the role of dealer was passed from player to player.

Legal or not, 21 became extremely popular thanks to two new rules that made it significantly more tempting as they notably reduced the dealer's advantage: the player could finally see one of the dealer's card before deciding whether to play and the dealer also had to follow precise rules when deciding whether to stand or hit, which the players were already aware of. It was the birth of the game as we know it today.

The name Blackjack derived from a new rule that emerged during the First World War and which anticipated a very lucky combination that paid out at 10:1: an Ace and a Jack, both of spades. The combination that made Blackjack and the relative odds would change more than once however, over the years, until taking the current form.

The game really took off in the Fifties and Sixties, when mathematicians and professional players began to develop the first strategies that aimed to reduce the advantage of the casino by using statistics and probability calculation. One pioneer was Roger Baldwin, who provided the first real strategy that could be used by the players directly. The idea came to him when he was a soldier, playing with his brothers in arms Wilbert Cantey, James McDermott and Herbert Maisel. Thanks to an available army computer, in 1956 the four friends published an article entitled *The Optimum Strategy in Blackjack* in the *Journal of the American Statistical Association*. One year later, on the basis of this article, Baldwin produced the book *Playing Blackjack to Win: a New Strategy for the Game of 21*. The strategy explained contained some inaccuracies, but the essential elements were correct and the first strains of card-counting emerged (variations on the basic strategy on the basis of the last cards seen, for example). It was only in 2008, fifty years after the book was published, that the four friends were included in the Blackjack Hall of Fame with the caption: "Without these men, none of us would be here today."

The next steps were taken by Edward Oakley Thorp, a professor at UCLA. He refined Baldwin's studies and in 1962 wrote *Beat the Dealer*, still today the most famous book on Blackjack. It was the first appearance of the card-counting technique with the ten-count method, a complex technique that was difficult for the average player to use.
In 1963 the computer scientist Harvey Dubner presented a card-counting method based on the attribution of a value equal to +1 or -1 to each card, then the programmer Julian Braun optimised it and in 1966 Thorp included it in the second version of Beat the Dealer. The Hi-Lo (or High-Low) method was born, and is still a popular card-counting system today.

Beat the dealer

The original intuition was based on the fact that in Blackjack, unlike all other games of chance, the memory of past events influences future events, because played cards are put aside and cannot be dealt in subsequent hands.

Thorp realised that the player would be able to capitalise on a greater number of high cards in the deck and in fact his technique kept track of these high cards, so that the player might know when the deck was favourable to him and accordingly adjust his bets.

The calculations required were by no means simple. Baldwin had used a military computer and Thorp had an IBM 704 with Fortran.

Following the publication of his book, the casinos soon had to seek a remedy. Initially they changed the rules of the game, claiming the right to shuffle the cards at any point in the game. The dealers then became experts in card-counting themselves and reshuffled the deck every time it was favourable to the player. But the players didn't like this one bit and it all became a big waste of time (and therefore of money); so the old rules were brought back in, but the number of decks was increased, from 1 to 4, 6, or 8.

After these initial card-counting techniques came the idea of a group of people who acted together in an organised and coordinated method with the aim of cleaning out the casino. It was Al Francesco, also known as Frank Schipani or Frank Salerni, who started it all in the Seventies with the "big player team concept": expert counters sat at various game tables, keeping bets low until the deck became favourable, then at an opportune moment they gave a signal to the so-called "big players" who sat at the table and began to bet large sums of money. A lot could be won with this method. The teams also had to be very skilled to avoid detection; while it was not illegal to count cards, the casino had the right to remove or ban players as they liked… and let's just say that being caught entailed "unfortunate" consequences.

Keith Taft was also playing in the same period; he was a scientist who used a small computer at the tables (at the time there were still no laws banning the use of electronic instruments). Keith also collaborated with Al Francesco, creating teams of players equipped with these computers.

Another personality well-known for these epic deeds was Ken Uston, who joined Al Francesco's team in 1974 as a big player, but he "betrayed" his team in 1977 when he published the book *The Big Player*, which revealed how Al Francesco and his team had won enormous amounts of money in casinos all over the world.

Ken Uston

The time was ripe and soon groups of quick-witted and intelligent young people realised they could win millions playing Blackjack… and the phenomenon spread across the United States like wildfire.

In 1978 the first "MIT Team" was born. Their story, told in the 2002 novel *Blackjack Club* by Ben Mezrich, was the basis of the film *21*, directed by Robert Luketic in 2008. In reality the team consisted of a group of students from the Massachusetts Institute of Technology (MIT), Harvard and other East Coast colleges, who turned the casino world, and the game of Blackjack itself, upside down with their alternating players, teams and investors.

THE GAME

*The reader must be able to
understand the effect of each
rule and of each possible
variation.*

Beat the dealer (1962-1966)
Edward Thorp

THE RULES

Blackjack is played at special semi-circular tables; the dealer sits behind the table and up to seven players sit around the edge, each of whom plays alone against the dealer. Usually six normal decks of 52 cards are used, which are well shuffled and then dealt from the shoe, the special device, also known as the sabot in other games, which deals cards one by one.

Picture cards are worth 10 points, the Ace can be worth 1 or 11 at the player's discretion and the other cards are worth their face value. The aim of the game is to achieve a total score, by adding up the value of your cards, that is greater than the dealer's, but without going over 21.

Before receiving their cards, players place a bet by placing their chips in the special betting space; the bet can be of any amount within the minimum and maximum limits of the table. When all bets have been made and the dealer announces "rien ne va plus", no further bets can be added, moved or removed.

The dealer distributes one card face-up to each player and one to himself; then a further card face-up to the players, but not to himself. Having assessed the sum of their two cards one by one the players, starting from the player to the dealer's left, can request one or more further cards (one at a time) with the intention of reaching or getting as close as possible to 21, or they might decide to "stand", which means stopping at the score achieved without requesting more cards. Anyone who goes over 21 "goes bust" and the dealer collects the bet.

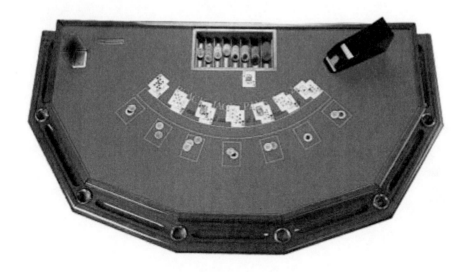

If your hand contains an Ace which can be counted as 11 without going bust, the total is known as "soft", all other hands are known instead as "hard". For example 7+8 and K+3+A are hard, while 5+2+A and 2+A+7 are soft.

Once all the players have played their hand, the dealer takes his second card and is then obliged to draw more cards until he goes over 16; but when he has 17 or over he must stand, meaning he can no longer hit.

At the end the dealer compares his score with those of each player: if his is higher, he wins and takes the bet, if his is less he pays out equal to the wager and in the case of a tied score the hand is null and void and the bet is simply returned to the player. Of course, if the dealer goes bust he loses against all the players remaining in the game and pays their bets equal to the wager.

If a player gets "blackjack" (or natural), meaning a total of 21 with just 2 cards (an Ace and any card with a value of 10), the dealer pays one and a half times the wager, unless he also got blackjack on his turn, in which case the hand is null and void.

Players normally bet in the betting space in front of them, but if there are other spaces free they can bet in them too.

Bets are also permitted where another player has already made a bet, but only the first player can control the hand and the second player cannot reprove him in any way for the way he played.

Once a hand is finished the dealer collects all the used cards and places them in the appropriate box; then a new hand is played in the same manner as the first. The deck is never finished however, in fact as a rule it is cut with a special plastic cutting card: when this is exposed all the cards are reshuffled.

A PLAYED HAND

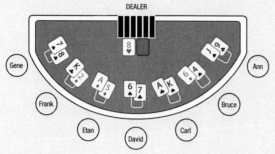

The dealer shows an 8.

• Ann has 19 and stands.

• Bruce has 10 and naturally hits; he gets a 2, hits again and receives a queen which takes him to 22.

• Carl has blackjack.

• David has 13 and correctly hits; he receives a 2 and stands (but he should have hit again against the dealer's 8 as we will see later).

• Etan has 16, but his Ace can count as 1 and so there is no risk of going bust; therefore he hits and receives a 5 which takes her to 21, the maximum.

• Frank has 12 and hits, he receives a 6 and stops at 18.

• Gene has 15 and quite rightly hits, he receives a 4 and stops at 19.

• The dealer turns over his second card, a 10, which takes him to 18 and, as per the rules, he stops.

• The dealer beats Bruce and David (and takes their bets), he draws with Frank (returns his bet) and loses against four players: Ann, Carl, Etan and Gene (he pays Carl, who got blackjack, one and a half times his wager).

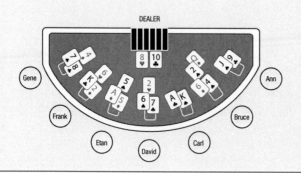

PLAYER OPTIONS

There are some other options that players might use in certain game situations: doubling down, splitting and insurance.

The fact is that these options have numerous variations. There is no standard rule, instead every casino, or rather, every single table, applies what they believe. We deem the rules that are used in the majority of European casinos to be standard, but we will also analyse the main variations.

Double down

Having received his first two cards and seen the dealer's first card, the player can decide to double down his bet, no matter what the initial two cards are. The downside is that if the player doubles down he receives one card, and one card only, from the dealer.

If other players have bet on the player who doubles down, they are not obliged to double down themselves, but they must nevertheless accept the attribution of just one card.

Let us examine an example. The player has 6-5 against the dealer's 7: if he doubles down and receives a 10 he obtains an unbeatable 21, but he might receive a 2 instead which stops him at a modest 13.

Split

When the player receives two initial cards of equal value he can decide to split them and consider them as two separate hands. This is how it works: the two equal cards are separated and the player places a bet equal to his original bet before each. The dealer distributes a second card to each of the two original cards and the two hands are played separately, one after the other. Picture cards are all considered to be worth 10 and any two cards worth 10 can be split (but this is never to your advantage).

For example, the player has 8-8 against the dealer's 9 and decides to split. He receives a 6 for the first 8 which takes him to 14: an insignificant total against the dealer's 9, so he hits again; the card is dealt and he goes bust so the dealer takes the bet. For the second 8 he receives an Ace, which takes the total to 19, a good number to stand on. The dealer draws another 9 and therefore loses with a total of 18 against the player's 19.

One bet lost and one won.

If, having split, the player receives another card of the same value, it is normally permitted to split the pair again and this process can be repeated up to four times.

In the rules that we deem standard, the player, having split and received the second card, cannot double down in any of the split hands.

A specific rule is applied to pairs of Aces. A player that receives two Aces can split them in the same way as a normal pair, but can then only receive one other card per hand (so he will close both hands with just two cards) and what is more, he cannot split again if he receives another Ace. Moreover if the second card is a 10 the score is deemed a normal 21 and not blackjack. During a split the decisions of the "controlling" player are binding for any other players who have bet on his hand.

Insurance

When the dealer's first card is an Ace, players can choose to insure themselves against the possibility of the dealer getting blackjack. In this case they make an extra bet (normally equal to half of the original bet) that is paid 2:1. In practice, if the dealer gets blackjack he pays the extra bet twice, otherwise he takes it. In any case, the player plays his hand against the dealer.

The decision to take insurance is not bound to the choice of the controlling player.

It is not wise to lose too much time over this option because it is almost never advantageous. It is essentially a bet that a card worth 10 will be dealt and that the dealer will therefore have blackjack. Considering that there are 16 cards with a value of 10 in every 52, in order for the bet to be fair it should be paid 36:16, or 9:4, a good deal more than the 2:1 offered; the dealer keeps a margin of approximately 8%. However this approximation does not have absolute value since, depending on the cards dealt, the remaining deck might be more or less full of 10s. Those who count the dealt cards might find themselves in situations in which taking insurance is actually advantageous to the player.

Bet variations

As well as the right to double down, split and take insurance, the player has another weapon up his sleeve. From hand to hand he can decide to vary his bet, increasing it when the situation becomes advantageous (we will see how in the advanced strategy chapter) and decreasing it when it becomes disadvantageous; this essentially means winning more when you win and losing less when you lose.

VARIATIONS

As we mentioned previously, there are many rules that vary from casino to casino and often from table to table within the same casino. These variations are sometimes decisive in choosing which strategy to adopt, it is therefore very important that each player is well-informed about the rules before sitting at a table, so as not to run into unfortunate misunderstandings that might cost him money.

As well as affecting which strategy to adopt, each variation also alters the advantage of the casino, sometimes positively, sometimes negatively; further on, in the advanced strategy chapter, we will see by exactly how much, in percentages, playing with a certain variation influences the dealer's profit margin.

Dealing
The dealer does not always deal a single card to himself (European no hole card rule). In fact in American, and some European, casinos the dealer takes two cards straight away, one face-up and the other face-down. If the up card is a 10 or Ace, the dealer checks whether the second card makes blackjack, obviously without showing it to the players. It is at this point that he takes insurance bets and then, if he has blackjack, declares it. This rule is advantageous for players as they discover straight away whether the dealer has blackjack without losing money by deciding to double down or split.

Number of decks
As a rule blackjack is played with 6 decks, but you will find tables with 4 to 8 decks or even tables where you play with 1 or 2 decks. The fewer decks there are, the more advantageous it is for the player who applies advanced strategies, in fact he can effectively use card-counting techniques.

Double down
In some casinos doubling down is only permitted if the total of the first two cards is 9, 10 or 11, in others it is only permitted with 10 and 11. Of course the less choice the player has, the more he is at a disadvantage.

Split

If, having split a pair, the player receives another card of equal value, in some casinos he can also split the new pair, but it is very rare that players are permitted to re-split Aces. On some tables it is permitted to double down after a split. These variations are favourable to the player.

Surrender

Some casinos allow surrender, which gives the players a chance to stop playing and retrieve half of their bet once they have seen the initial cards dealt. There are two different types: early surrender and late surrender. With the latter players can only surrender after the dealer has checked whether he has blackjack. Almost no casino in the world still permits early surrender, as it gives players too much of an advantage, while late surrender is mostly allowed in casinos in Asia and the Caribbean. Since late surrender means that the player can surrender only after the dealer has checked that he hasn't made blackjack, this option is not offered in the majority of European casinos, where the no hole card rule is used instead, as this implies that the dealer will check whether he has blackjack only after the last player has finished his turn.

17 soft

In some casinos the dealer has to stand with a hard 17, while with a soft 17 he is obliged to hit.

BASIC STRATEGY

Players, for some strange reason, tend
not to make the decisions most favourable to them,
only to then bemoan the bad luck that follows them.

Dario De Toffoli and Margherita Bonaldi

CORRECT DECISIONS

The Blackjack player must constantly make decisions.

First of all, he must learn when to hit and when to stand, and should never act on impulse - there are tables that show the best move for every single game situation. These are tables that have been compiled with the utmost accuracy, applying the theory of probability to each situation. Any decision other than that suggested in the table will only reduce the chances of winning. And of course the purpose of the game is precisely the opposite: to maximise the chances of winning in the long run.

The Blackjack player must then learn to exploit the options offered by the casino, such as doubling down and splitting: only then can he hope to compete with the dealer. Here again, he must never trust his feelings, but quite simply follow the tables which show the statistically most productive action to take in each situation. The reality is that the majority of players don't pay attention to the tables, lose and then bemoan their misfortune, rather than their irrational behaviour. These are dream clients for the casinos!

There is no room for imagination in Blackjack! Anyone wanting to give free rein to their creativity is better off playing Poker. Blackjack is an entirely mechanical game! It is interesting, complex, appealing, fun… but completely mechanical. It's a game that is "resolved" by mathematics as it were, and anyone who ignores the maths is quite simply wrong.

In other words, a "basic strategy" has been developed using the probability theory, which allows the player to play as best as possible in every situation, only taking his own cards and the dealer's up card into account. This strategy can be summed up in a series of tables that show the most advantageous decision for the player in all possible game situations.

We show these tables over the following pages with the warning that in some cases the strategy may vary according to the specific rules of a casino.

The strategy proposed here refers specifically to Blackjack played by the following rules:

- It is played with six decks;
- The "no hole card rule" is in force, meaning the dealer only looks at his second card after all players have played their hands;
- The dealer must stand on soft 17;
- No doubling down is permitted after a split.

HIT vs. STAND TABLE

HARD HANDS: DEALER'S UP CARD

PLAYER	2	3	4	5	6	7	8	9	10	A
11/-	HIT	HIT	HIT	HIT	HIT	HIT	HIT	HIT	HIT	HIT
12	HIT	HIT	STAND	STAND	STAND	HIT	HIT	HIT	HIT	HIT
13	STAND	STAND	STAND	STAND	STAND	HIT	HIT	HIT	HIT	HIT
14	STAND	STAND	STAND	STAND	STAND	HIT	HIT	HIT	HIT	HIT
15	STAND	STAND	STAND	STAND	STAND	HIT	HIT	HIT	HIT	HIT
16	STAND	STAND	STAND	STAND	STAND	HIT	HIT	HIT	HIT	HIT
17/+	STAND	STAND	STAND	STAND	STAND	STAND	STAND	STAND	STAND	STAND

SOFT HANDS: DEALER'S UP CARD

PLAYER	2	3	4	5	6	7	8	9	10	A
17/-	HIT	HIT	HIT	HIT	HIT	HIT	HIT	HIT	HIT	HIT
18	STAND	STAND	STAND	STAND	STAND	STAND	STAND	HIT	HIT	HIT
19	STAND	STAND	STAND	STAND	STAND	STAND	STAND	STAND	STAND	STAND

The rows contain the total of the player's cards, the columns show the dealer's up card. So always hit with totals of up to 11 and always stand with totals of 17 or greater. Only when the player has a total between 12 and 16 does the choice depend on the dealer's card.

For example, hit with 12 if the dealer has a 3, but stand if it has a 4.

For example, stand with 16 if the dealer has a 6, but hit if he has a 7. Trust me, I know many players stand with 16, but that is a mistake.

The second table shows the game situations in which the player has a "soft" total, meaning he has an Ace in hand that can count as 11 without making him go bust.

Here too the rows contain the player's total and the columns the dealer's up card.

The player should always hit with a "soft" total that is less or equal to 17 (we will see later that in some cases it is also advantageous to double down), while with a total greater than 18 it is best to stand. Only a total of 18 presents different options: only hit against the dealer's 9, 10 or Ace (this is intuitive since with these initial cards the dealer has a high probability of achieving a total greater than 18, as 4 out of 13 cards have a value of 10).

DOUBLE DOWN TABLE

DEALER'S UP CARD

PLAYER	2	3	4	5	6	7	8	9	10	A
8/-										
9		DD	DD	DD	DD					
10	DD	DD	DD	DD	DD	DD	DD	DD		
11	DD	DD	DD	DD	DD	DD	DD	DD		
12/+										
A+2				DD	DD					
A+3				DD	DD					
A+4			DD	DD	DD					
A+5			DD	DD	DD					
A+6		DD	DD	DD	DD					
A+7		DD	DD	DD	DD					
A+8										
A+9										

This table shows when it is appropriate to double down.

In the columns we have the possible values of the dealer's up card and in the rows the possible totals of the player, after the first two cards.

While many casinos allow doubling down with any total, obviously it is only advantageous to do so in some cases, because having doubled down the player will receive one card and one card only. To be specific, it is ill-advised with all "hard" totals of less than 9 or greater 11, while for players with 9, 10 or 11 in hand it becomes an excellent option.

With a 10 for example, the player must almost always double down, provided that the dealer does not also have a 10, or an Ace.

But, when the player has an Ace in hand, he must not double down if the other card is greater than 7, because in this case he already has an excellent 19 at least and receiving another card would most likely obtain a worse result. However, in other cases it is sometimes the best move; for example, double down with A-5 in hand if the dealer has 4, 5 or 6, while with A-3 only double down if the dealer has 5 or 6.

SPLIT TABLE

DEALER'S UP CARD

PLAYER	2	3	4	5	6	7	8	9	10	A
2+2			SPLIT	SPLIT	SPLIT	SPLIT				
3+3			SPLIT	SPLIT	SPLIT	SPLIT				
4+4										
5+5										
6+6		SPLIT	SPLIT	SPLIT	SPLIT					
7+7	SPLIT	SPLIT	SPLIT	SPLIT	SPLIT	SPLIT				
8+8	SPLIT	SPLIT	SPLIT.	SPLIT	SPLIT	SPLIT	SPLIT	SPLIT		
9+9	SPLIT	SPLIT	SPLIT	SPLIT	SPLIT		SPLIT	SPLIT		
10+10										
A+A	SPLIT	SPLIT	SPLIT	SPLIT	SPLIT	SPLIT	SPLIT	SPLIT	SPLIT	

This table shows when the player must split an initial pair of cards of equal value.

The rows show the possible pairs and the columns the value of the dealer's up card. We see that you never split with 4-4, 5-5 or 10-10, whereas in other cases splitting is very often an advantageous option. For example, with a pair of 7's we split if the dealer has a total of between 2 and 7, but not if the dealer has an 8, 9, 10 or Ace. With 9-9 we split unless the dealer has a 7, 10 or Ace (because the most probable card, 10, brings us to a total of 19 if we split, which is better than the 18 in hand).

GENERAL TABLE

DEALER'S UP CARD

PLAYER	2	3	4	5	6	7	8	9	10	A
7/-	HIT	HIT	HIT	HIT	HIT	HIT	HIT	HIT	HIT	HIT
8	HIT	HIT	HIT	HIT	HIT	HIT	HIT	HIT	HIT	HIT
9	HIT	DD	DD	DD	DD	HIT	HIT	HIT	HIT	HIT
10	DD	DD	DD	DD	DD	DD	DD	DD	HIT	HIT
11	DD	DD	DD	DD	DD	DD	DD	DD	HIT	HIT
12	HIT	HIT	STAND	STAND	STAND	HIT	HIT	HIT	HIT	HIT
13	STAND	STAND	STAND	STAND	STAND	HIT	HIT	HIT	HIT	HIT
14	STAND	STAND	STAND	STAND	STAND	HIT	HIT	HIT	HIT	HIT
15	STAND	STAND	STAND	STAND	STAND	HIT	HIT	HIT	HIT	HIT
16	STAND	STAND	STAND	STAND	STAND	HIT	HIT	HIT	HIT	HIT
17/+	STAND	STAND	STAND	STAND	STAND	STAND	STAND	STAND	STAND	STAND
A+2	HIT	HIT	HIT	DD	DD	HIT	HIT	HIT	HIT	HIT
A+3	HIT	HIT	HIT	DD	DD	HIT	HIT	HIT	HIT	HIT
A+4	HIT	HIT	DD	DD	DD	HIT	HIT	HIT	HIT	HIT
A+5	HIT	HIT	DD	DD	DD	HIT	HIT	HIT	HIT	HIT
A+6	HIT	DD	DD	DD	DD	HIT	HIT	HIT	HIT	HIT
A+7	STAND	DD	DD	DD	DD	STAND	STAND	HIT	HIT	HIT
A+8	STAND	STAND	STAND	STAND	STAND	STAND	STAND	STAND	STAND	STAND
A+9	STAND	STAND	STAND	STAND	STAND	STAND	STAND	STAND	STAND	STAND
2+2	HIT	HIT	SPLIT	SPLIT	SPLIT	SPLIT	HIT	HIT	HIT	HIT
3+3	HIT	HIT	SPLIT	SPLIT	SPLIT	SPLIT	HIT	HIT	HIT	HIT
4+4	HIT	HIT	HIT	HIT	HIT	HIT	HIT	HIT	HIT	HIT
5+5	DD	DD	DD	DD	DD	DD	DD	DD	HIT	HIT
6+6	HIT	SPLIT	SPLIT	SPLIT	SPLIT	HIT	HIT	HIT	HIT	HIT
7+7	SPLIT	SPLIT	SPLIT	SPLIT	SPLIT	SPLIT	HIT	HIT	HIT	HIT
8+8	SPLIT	SPLIT	SPLIT.	SPLIT	SPLIT	SPLIT	SPLIT	SPLIT	HIT	HIT
9+9	SPLIT	SPLIT	SPLIT	SPLIT	SPLIT	STAND	SPLIT	SPLIT	STAND	STAND
10+10	STAND	STAND	STAND	STAND	STAND	STAND	STAND	STAND	STAND	STAND
A+A	SPLIT	SPLIT	SPLIT	SPLIT	SPLIT	SPLIT	SPLIT	SPLIT	SPLIT	HIT

THE EFFECTS OF GAME VARIATIONS

As explained in the chapter on the rules of the game, the adoption of some game variations can modify the strategy, sometimes significantly.

There are two rules in particular that play an important role in defining a correct strategy: the "no hole card rule" and whether or not doubling down is allowed after a split.

In general, the game is played in Europe with the "no hole card rule", which means the dealer draws the second card only after players have played their hands; the basic idea is that if the dealer shows an Ace or 10, the player cannot exclude the possibility that it may have blackjack and so plays less aggressively. In America on the other hand, the dealer generally draws his second card straight away and checks whether he has blackjack before the players make their decisions.

The other important rule is the possibility of doubling down after a split; when this is permitted players must split more often in order to make the most of the advantageous opportunities to double down that may arise following a split.

Let's see which strategies are influenced by these particular rules.

Double down without the no hole card rule
The only difference to the normal strategy occurs when the player has 11 against the dealer's 10: in this case he should double down.

DEALER'S UP CARD

	2	3	4	5	6	7	8	9	10	A
9		DD	DD	DD	DD					
10	DD	DD	DD	DD	DD	DD	DD	DD		
11	DD	DD	DD	DD	DD	DD	DD	DD	DD	
A+2				DD	DD					
A+3				DD	DD					
A+4			DD	DD	DD					
A+5			DD	DD	DD					
A+6		DD	DD	DD	DD					
A+7		DD	DD	DD	DD					

PLAYER

Split without the no hole card rule

In this case the difference in strategy occurs when faced with the dealer's 10 and Ace, against which pairs of 8's and Aces are also split, because the player can be more aggressive. It follows that pairs of 8's and Aces are always split.

DEALER'S UP CARD

PLAYER	2	3	4	5	6	7	8	9	10	A
2+2			SPLIT	SPLIT	SPLIT	SPLIT				
3+3			SPLIT	SPLIT	SPLIT	SPLIT				
4+4										
5+5										
6+6		SPLIT	SPLIT	SPLIT	SPLIT					
7+7	SPLIT	SPLIT	SPLIT	SPLIT	SPLIT	SPLIT				
8+8	SPLIT	SPLIT	SPLIT.	SPLIT	SPLIT	SPLIT	SPLIT	SPLIT	SPLIT	SPLIT
9+9	SPLIT	SPLIT	SPLIT	SPLIT	SPLIT		SPLIT	SPLIT		
10+10										
A+A	SPLIT	SPLIT	SPLIT	SPLIT	SPLIT	SPLIT	SPLIT	SPLIT	SPLIT	SPLIT

Split with double down after split

Here there are numerous differences to the normal strategy, meaning there are more cases in which splitting gains a little mathematical expectation.

• Pairs of 2's and 3's against the dealer's 2 or 3;
• Pair of 4's against the dealer's 5 or 6;
• Pair of 6's against the dealer's 2.

DEALER'S UP CARD

PLAYER	2	3	4	5	6	7	8	9	10	A
2+2	SPLIT	SPLIT	SPLIT	SPLIT	SPLIT	SPLIT				
3+3	SPLIT	SPLIT	SPLIT	SPLIT	SPLIT	SPLIT				
4+4				SPLIT	SPLIT					
5+5										
6+6	SPLIT	SPLIT	SPLIT	SPLIT	SPLIT					
7+7	SPLIT	SPLIT	SPLIT	SPLIT	SPLIT	SPLIT				
8+8	SPLIT	SPLIT	SPLIT.	SPLIT	SPLIT	SPLIT	SPLIT	SPLIT		
9+9	SPLIT	SPLIT	SPLIT	SPLIT	SPLIT		SPLIT	SPLIT		
10+10										
A+A	SPLIT	SPLIT	SPLIT	SPLIT	SPLIT	SPLIT	SPLIT	SPLIT	SPLIT	

Split without no hole card rule and with double down after split

If both variations are permitted, the strategy combines the effects of both.

DEALER'S UP CARD

		2	3	4	5	6	7	8	9	10	A
PLAYER	2+2	SPLIT	SPLIT	SPLIT	SPLIT	SPLIT	SPLIT				
	3+3	SPLIT	SPLIT	SPLIT	SPLIT	SPLIT	SPLIT				
	4+4				SPLIT	SPLIT					
	5+5										
	6+6	SPLIT	SPLIT	SPLIT	SPLIT	SPLIT					
	7+7	SPLIT	SPLIT	SPLIT	SPLIT	SPLIT	SPLIT				
	8+8	SPLIT	SPLIT	SPLIT.	SPLIT	SPLIT	SPLIT	SPLIT	SPLIT	SPLIT	SPLIT
	9+9	SPLIT	SPLIT	SPLIT	SPLIT	SPLIT		SPLIT	SPLIT		
	10+10										
	A+A	SPLIT	SPLIT	SPLIT	SPLIT	SPLIT	SPLIT	SPLIT	SPLIT	SPLIT	SPLIT

Surrender

The player should choose early surrender in the following cases:

1. Dealer A – player 17, 16, 15, 13, 12, 7, 6, 5
2. Dealer 10 – player 16, 15, 14

The player's totals are hard.

Where late surrender is possible (it is incompatible with the no hole card rule) and permitted, let's see when it is advantageous to use this rule.

It is better to surrender (and lose half of the bet) in the few situations in which playing would mean losing on average more than half of the bets, despite making the best decisions, i.e. if the mathematical hope were less than -0.50 regardless. These situations are listed here:

3. Player 15 – dealer 10: Better to surrender than hit
4. Player 16 hard – dealer 9: Better to surrender than hit
5. Player 16 hard – dealer 10: Better to surrender than hit
6. Player 16 hard – dealer A: Better to surrender than hit
7. Player 8+8 – dealer 10: Better to surrender than hit

THE MATHS BEHIND THE GAME: THE DEALER

Well, now we've seen the tables, which can actually be found in many international texts dedicated to Blackjack.

However, what's not so easy to find is a mathematical explanation for these tables, i.e. how they are calculated.

That is perhaps why many players are mistrustful of the strategies found in books, why they do not believe that mathematics can tell them how to play.

Allow us then to demonstrate the validity of these tables by recalculating them item by item and giving examples of the various calculation methods (trying not to bore you with endless pages of formulas and calculations!).

In order to carry out a probabilistic analysis of Blackjack, it is necessary to study the two participating figures: the dealer and the player.

The fundamental difference between them is that the dealer's behaviour is forced (he must hit until he reaches a total of 17 or greater), whereas the player is constantly making decisions.

Firstly we will calculate the probability of the dealer obtaining the various possible totals starting from its up card; then, considering the player's first two cards, we will see how the possibilities of winning, losing or drawing vary depending on his choices. The most advantageous move can be determined by comparing the results.

THE INFINITE DECK APPROXIMATION

The number of decks in use is variable and consequently the probability calculation varies from case to case, because the probability of a card being drawn varies once others have already been drawn.

But by how much does it vary?

Is it legitimate to make a general calculation that can be applied in all situations? Or is that too great a deviation from the real situation?

We will try to answer this conundrum.

Firstly, we used the simplest method for the calculations, applying what we have called "the infinite deck approximation".

This means that we assume we are always playing with a dealer's shoe containing infinite decks, so that every card has the same probability of being drawn as the others, that is, 1 out of 13, except 10, which has a probability of 4/13 as four of the cards are worth 10.

In reality, if playing with a finite number of decks (e.g. 6) the cards that have already been drawn influence the probability of the next cards being drawn.

If, when playing with a single deck, the 9 has already been drawn out of seven up cards, the real probability that the next card is another 9 is 3/45 (in the deck there are still 45 cards of which three are 9), somewhat different to the theoretical 1/13 of the infinite deck. It should be noted that it is precisely on these probabilistic deviations that advanced strategies are based, which are applied by counting the cards as they are drawn.

Once we had made the calculations with the infinite deck, we then examined a series of real cases and the deviation observed was always very modest (generally less than 0.5%) and therefore much smaller than the differences in probability caused as a result of the player's different choices. In other words, using the infinite deck approximation does not influence the final results in that it does not lead to any variation in the player's actual choices.

Therefore the following treatise uses the infinite deck approximation.

The dealer's chances

And now it's the dealer's turn. We see his first card and the six possible totals are 17, 18, 19, 20, 21 and 22/+, where 22/+ includes all the values for which the dealer goes bust.

The first calculation to be made is the dealer's outcome probabilities, or the dealer's chances of obtaining each of the six possible totals, starting from every possible first card.

We will calculate what is known in probability theory as conditional probability, or the dealer's chances of obtaining a determined total subject to knowing the value of its first card.

The results are summarised in the following table.

DEALER'S FINAL TOTALS

		17	18	19	20	21	>21
	2	13.98	13.49	12.97	12.40	11.80	35.36
	3	13.50	13.05	12.56	12.03	11.47	37.39
	4	13.05	12.59	12.14	11.65	11.12	39.45
	5	12.23	12.23	11.77	11.31	10.82	41.64
DEALER'S UP CARD	**6**	16.54	10.63	10.63	10.17	9.72	42.32
	7	36.86	13.78	7.86	7.86	7.41	26.23
	8	12.86	35.93	12.86	6.94	6.94	24.47
	9	12.00	12.00	35.08	12.00	6.08	22.84
	10	11.14	11.14	11.14	34.22	11.14	21.21
	A	13.08	13.08	13.08	13.08	36.15	11.52

The data is shown in percentages, %

Dealer sequences with an exposed 10

We will now see how these calculations were made, by examining one of the simplest examples: the dealer's up card is a 10.

With an initial 10, each total can be obtained in several ways, that is, with different sequences of cards; a second card may be sufficient (e.g. 10+8=18), or two cards might be needed (10+3+10=22/+), or three (10+4+A+2=17) or even more if the dealer turns over a series of low-value cards. The tree diagram on the next page shows the different possible combinations.

When a sequence of cards gives us a total that we have already examined, the table refers us to that continuation for simplicity's sake. For example if the sequence of cards is 10-5-A, we have 16 and the continuation is considered identical to the continuation that would occur with 16 from two cards. The tree diagram gives an idea of all the dealer's possible card sequences when his first card is 10.

FIRST CARD	SECOND CARD		THIRD CARD	
10+	A	= 21 STOP!		
	10	= 20 STOP!		
	9	= 19 STOP!		
	8	= 18 STOP!		
	7	= 17 STOP!		
	6	= 16 +	A	= 17 STOP!
			2	= 18 STOP!
			3	= 19 STOP!
			4	= 20 STOP!
			5	= 21 STOP!
			6, 7, 8, 9, 10	= >21 STOP!
	5	= 15 +	A	= 16 + ...
			2	= 17 STOP!
			3	= 18 STOP!
			4	= 19 STOP!
			5	= 20 STOP!
			6	= 21 STOP!
			7, 8, 9, 10	= >21 STOP!
	4	= 14 +	A	= 15 + ...
			2	= 16 + ...
			3	= 17 STOP!
			4	= 18 STOP!
			5	= 19 STOP!
			6	= 20 STOP!
			7	= 21 STOP!
			8, 9, 10	= >21 STOP!
	3	= 13 +	A	= 14 + ...
			2	= 15 + ...
			3	= 16 + ...
			4	= 17 STOP!
			5	= 18 STOP!
			6	= 19 STOP!
			7	= 20 STOP!
			8	= 21 STOP!
			9, 10	= >21 STOP!
	2	= 12 +	A	= 13 + ...
			2	= 14 + ...
			3	= 15 + ...
			4	= 16 + ...
			5	= 17 STOP!
			6	= 18 STOP!
			7	= 19 STOP!
			8	= 20 STOP!
			9	= 21 STOP!
			10	= > 21 STOP!

In order to better illustrate the calculation, let us examine the only case in which the dealer gets a total of 20 (still with 10 as the first card) and see how probable it is that this will occur.

For example, when the first card is a 10, 20 can be obtained by drawing another 10 or drawing a 3 and then a 7, but watch out, 20 cannot be obtained by drawing first a 7 and then a 3 because 10+7=17 and the dealer is forced to stand; or again, the dealer might draw a 2, a 4 and then another 4, or rather a 3, a 2 and a 5, etc.

The following table summarises all these possibilities in order and shows the relative probability next to them.

For example, the probability of obtaining 20 with two cards by drawing another 10 straight away is 4/13, as four out of thirteen cards are worth 10; the probability of getting 20 by drawing a 3 and a 7 is 1/13x1/13, that is, the probability of drawing a 3 as the second card (1/13) multiplied by the probability of drawing 7 as the third card (1/13 again).

There are many combinations and they are all shown in the following table, alongside the relative probabilities.

The probability of getting 20 with only two cards is 4/13 (there is only one sequence: 10-10). To get 20 with three cards there are five different sequences, so the probability is 5x1/13x1/13. And so on.

Obviously combinations with a greater number of cards are less likely, precisely because the probability of a series of extractions is equal to the product of the probabilities of the individual extractions.

In order to obtain the total probability of the dealer obtaining 20 starting with a 10, it suffices to add up all the probabilities in the table:

$$P_{tot} = 4/13 + 5/13^2 + 10/13^3 + 10/13^4 + 5/13^5 + 1/13^6 = 34.22\%$$

This corresponds exactly to the value in the corresponding field in the table of the dealer's outcome probabilities.

DEALER TOTAL 20 FROM AN EXPOSED 10

DEALER'S CARD							PROBABILITY
I	II	III	VI	V	VI	VII	
10	10						4/13
	6	4					1/13 x 1/13
	5	5					1/13 x 1/13
	4	6					1/13 x 1/13
	3	7					1/13 x 1/13
	2	8					1/13 x 1/13
	5	1	4				1/13 x 1/13 x 1/13
	4	2	4				1/13 x 1/13 x 1/13
	4	1	5				1/13 x 1/13 x 1/13
	3	3	4				1/13 x 1/13 x 1/13
	3	2	5				1/13 x 1/13 x 1/13
	3	1	6				1/13 x 1/13 x 1/13
	2	4	4				1/13 x 1/13 x 1/13
	2	3	5				1/13 x 1/13 x 1/13
	2	2	6				1/13 x 1/13 x 1/13
	2	1	7				1/13 x 1/13 x 1/13
	4	1	1	4			1/13 x 1/13 x 1/13 x 1/13
	3	2	1	4			1/13 x 1/13 x 1/13 x 1/13
	3	1	2	4			1/13 x 1/13 x 1/13 x 1/13
	3	1	1	5			1/13 x 1/13 x 1/13 x 1/13
	2	3	1	4			1/13 x 1/13 x 1/13 x 1/13
	2	2	2	4			1/13 x 1/13 x 1/13 x 1/13
	2	2	1	5			1/13 x 1/13 x 1/13 x 1/13
	2	1	3	4			1/13 x 1/13 x 1/13 x 1/13
	2	1	2	5			1/13 x 1/13 x 1/13 x 1/13
	2	1	1	6			1/13 x 1/13 x 1/13 x 1/13
	3	1	1	1	4		1/13 x 1/13 x 1/13 x 1/13 x 1/13
	2	2	1	1	4		1/13 x 1/13 x 1/13 x 1/13 x 1/13
	2	1	2	1	4		1/13 x 1/13 x 1/13 x 1/13 x 1/13
	2	1	1	2	4		1/13 x 1/13 x 1/13 x 1/13 x 1/13
	2	1	1	1	5		1/13 x 1/13 x 1/13 x 1/13 x 1/13
	2	1	1	1	1	4	1/13 x 1/13 x 1/13 x 1/13 x 1/13 x 1/13

Markov Chains

Let's simplify things.

We have seen how the dealer's chances of obtaining different totals (17, 18, 19, 20, 21, 22/+) are calculated. The likelihood of going from one total to another, with the extraction of a single card, is easily calculated. To go from 2 to 9 for example, the probability will be 1/13 (we need a 7); while to go from 2 to 12 it will be 4/13 (we need any card with a value of 10). On the other hand, going from 4 to 16 with the extraction of one card is impossible, so we have a probability of 0, just as for passing from 7 to 6. But since the final totals can be achieved through more than one extraction, the situation is complicated exponentially, forcing long and tedious manual calculations.

Fortunately mathematics supplies us with a model that is particularly useful as well as being simple and elegant: Markov Chains. These allow us to automate the calculations, making them much simpler; it suffices that you are able to handle some mathematical tools, matrices in particular.

A Markov chain is a mathematical model with the particular property that it describes a system through a succession of random variables.

This is exactly the case for the dealer's totals: the sequence of totals that the dealer obtains by drawing his cards one after the other is precisely a succession of random variables each dependent on the previous. The values vary because the card drawn is random, not predetermined; they are dependent, because the total obtained from hand to hand depends on the previous total.
If instead of the sum of the cards drawn, we were to consider only the value of the last one, there would be no dependence between one extraction and the next and it would not therefore be a Markov chain.

Essentially, in Blackjack the succession of partial sums obtained after each card is a Markov chain, because the values of the sequence are random and furthermore each extraction is dependent on the previous one. If the dealer receives 10-3-2-5 for example, the corresponding Markov chain is 10-13-15-20. This model can only be used because we are considering the infinite deck approximation meaning that at each extraction each card effectively has the same probability of being drawn as the others and there is no memory effect.

What distinguishes the Markov chain from other models of this type is in fact this absence of memory (or Markov property), according to which the future state of a Markov chain depends only on the present state (and not on its past history).
The total obtained after each extraction is called a state. Some of these states are particularly important in view of our study and are the so-called "absorbing states", which having been arrived at, are not abandoned (they put an end to the sequence); they are the states that correspond to the six final totals that can be

obtained by the dealer: 17, 18, 19, 20, 21 and 22/+.

We have seen that for every pair of states it is easy to calculate the probability of going from one to another in a single move (or rather, by drawing a single card), but things rapidly become complicated if the moves increase.

Markov chains come to our aid, as they enjoy certain properties that allow us to easily calculate the probability of obtaining a certain final total with any number of extractions, starting from any initial card.

In order to do this calculation it is necessary to use matrices. In our case the matrix is a table in which both the rows and columns are all possible states, while each field shows the probability of passing from the state in the row to the state in the column with a single draw. This is what we call the transition matrix (pg. 38).

For example, starting from 8 (row 8) there is a 7.69% (1/13) chance of reaching 17 (column 17) in a single draw; again, starting from 5 there is a 30.77% (4/13) chance of reaching 15 (column 15) in one draw; finally, starting from 9 there is a 0% chance of reaching 22/+ (column 22/+) in one draw.

Notations such as 3(13) should be understood as "soft" totals (an Ace with a 2 is a soft 13) and 22/+ as usual indicates totals greater than 21.

Thanks to the Markov property, by multiplying the transition matrix by itself we obtain the probability of going from one state to another with two draws. By multiplying once again the matrix obtained with the transition matrix we obtain the probability with three draws and so on. So it suffices to import our initial matrix, into an excel spreadsheet for example, to quickly find the dealer's outcome probabilities, instead of having to consider all the possible card combinations.

To understand how the method works we will try to explain the first step; if, for example, we want to find the probability of going from 4 to 12 with two draws, it is not enough to simply multiply the two numbers, instead it is necessary to use the whole row that corresponds to a total of 4 (the probability of going from 4 to all the other possible totals) and the whole column of total 12 (the probability of reaching 12 from all the possible totals with a single draw); once the corresponding row and column have been selected, the data sought will be the product of the first element in the row multiplied by the first in the column, plus the second element of the row multiplied by the second of the column, plus the third multiplied by the third and so on until the end. Let us examine this operation in detail.

TRANSITION MATRIX

	A(11)	2	2(12)	3	3(13)	4	4(14)	5	5(15)	6	6(16)	7	8	9	10	11	12	13	14	15	16	17	18	19	20	21	22+
A(11)	0	0	7.69	0	7.69	0	7.69	0	7.69	0	7.69	7.69	7.69	7.69	0	7.69	0	0	0	0	0	7.69	7.69	7.69	7.69	30.77	0
2	0	0	0	0	7.69	7.69	0	7.69	7.69	7.69	0	7.69	7.69	7.69	7.69	7.69	30.77	0	0	0	0	0	0	7.69	7.69	0	0
2(12)	7.69	0	0	0	7.69	0	7.69	0	7.69	0	7.69	7.69	7.69	7.69	7.69	7.69	30.77	30.77	0	0	0	0	0	0	0	0	0
3	0	0	7.69	0	7.69	0	7.69	0	7.69	0	7.69	7.69	7.69	7.69	7.69	0	30.77	30.77	0	0	0	0	0	0	0	7.69	0
3(13)	7.69	0	0	0	0	0	7.69	0	7.69	0	7.69	7.69	7.69	7.69	7.69	7.69	7.69	30.77	30.77	0	0	0	7.69	7.69	0	0	0
4	0	0	0	0	0	7.69	0	7.69	0	7.69	0	7.69	7.69	7.69	7.69	7.69	7.69	30.77	30.77	0	0	0	7.69	7.69	0	0	0
4(14)	0	0	0	0	0	0	0	0	0	0	7.69	7.69	7.69	7.69	7.69	7.69	7.69	7.69	30.77	30.77	0	0	7.69	7.69	7.69	7.69	0
5	0	0	0	0	0	0	0	0	0	0	7.69	7.69	7.69	0	0	0	7.69	7.69	30.77	30.77	0	0	7.69	7.69	7.69	7.69	0
5(15)	0	0	0	0	0	0	0	0	0	0	7.69	0	7.69	7.69	7.69	0	7.69	7.69	7.69	30.77	30.77	7.69	7.69	0	7.69	7.69	0
6	0	0	0	0	0	0	0	0	0	0	0	0	0	0	0	7.69	7.69	7.69	7.69	30.77	30.77	7.69	7.69	7.69	7.69	7.69	0
6(16)	0	0	0	0	0	0	0	0	0	0	0	0	0	7.69	7.69	7.69	7.69	7.69	7.69	7.69	30.77	7.69	30.77	7.69	7.69	7.69	0
7	0	0	0	0	0	0	0	0	0	0	0	0	0	7.69	0	7.69	7.69	7.69	7.69	7.69	7.69	30.77	7.69	7.69	7.69	0	0
8	0	0	0	0	0	0	0	0	0	0	0	0	0	0	0	7.69	7.69	7.69	7.69	7.69	7.69	7.69	30.77	7.69	7.69	7.69	0
9	0	0	0	0	0	0	0	0	0	0	0	0	0	0	0	7.69	7.69	7.69	7.69	7.69	7.69	7.69	7.69	30.77	7.69	7.69	0
10	0	0	0	0	0	0	0	0	0	0	0	0	0	0	0	0	7.69	7.69	7.69	7.69	7.69	7.69	7.69	7.69	30.77	7.69	0
11	0	0	0	0	0	0	0	0	0	0	0	0	0	0	0	0	7.69	7.69	7.69	7.69	7.69	7.69	7.69	7.69	7.69	30.77	0
12	0	0	0	0	0	0	0	0	0	0	0	0	0	0	0	0	0	7.69	7.69	7.69	7.69	7.69	7.69	7.69	7.69	7.69	30.77
13	0	0	0	0	0	0	0	0	0	0	0	0	0	0	0	0	0	0	7.69	7.69	7.69	7.69	7.69	7.69	7.69	7.69	38.46
14	0	0	0	0	0	0	0	0	0	0	0	0	0	0	0	0	0	0	0	7.69	7.69	7.69	7.69	7.69	7.69	7.69	46.15
15	0	0	0	0	0	0	0	0	0	0	0	0	0	0	0	0	0	0	0	0	7.69	7.69	7.69	7.69	7.69	7.69	53.85
16	0	0	0	0	0	0	0	0	0	0	0	0	0	0	0	0	0	0	0	0	0	7.69	7.69	7.69	7.69	7.69	61.54
17	0	0	0	0	0	0	0	0	0	0	0	0	0	0	0	0	0	0	0	0	0	100	0	0	0	0	0
18	0	0	0	0	0	0	0	0	0	0	0	0	0	0	0	0	0	0	0	0	0	0	100	0	0	0	0
19	0	0	0	0	0	0	0	0	0	0	0	0	0	0	0	0	0	0	0	0	0	0	0	100	0	0	0
20	0	0	0	0	0	0	0	0	0	0	0	0	0	0	0	0	0	0	0	0	0	0	0	0	100	0	0
21	0	0	0	0	0	0	0	0	0	0	0	0	0	0	0	0	0	0	0	0	0	0	0	0	0	100	0
22+	0	0	0	0	0	0	0	0	0	0	0	0	0	0	0	0	0	0	0	0	0	0	0	0	0	0	100

The data is shown in percentages, %

In the table below, for each possible combination we find the percentage given by "row 4", by "column 12" and finally by the product of the two percentages, the combined percentage.

Each multiplication corresponds to the extraction of the next two cards, for example, multiplying the 5(15) field means calculating the probability of going from 4 to soft 5 (drawing an Ace in other words) and then from soft 5 to 12 (drawing a 7) and we obtain 7.69x7.69=0.59%.

Adding together all the probability products results in the value 4.14 (this too is a percentage, which will appear in the second level matrix at the intersection of row 4 and column 12.

PRODUCT TABLE

	ROW 4	COLUMN 12	PRODUCT
A(11)	0	0	0
2	0	30.77	0
2(12)	0	30.77	0
3	0	7.69	0
3(13)	0	7.69	0
4	0	7.69	0
4(14)	0	7.69	0
5	0	7.69	0
5(15)	7.69	7.69	0.59
6	7.69	7.69	0.59
6(16)	0	7.69	0
7	7.69	7.69	0.59
8	7.69	7.69	0.59
9	7.69	7.69	0.59
10	7.69	7.69	0.59
11	7.69	7.69	0.59
12	7.69	0	0
13	7.69	0	0
14	30.77	0	0
15	0	0	0
16	0	0	0
17	0	0	0
18	0	0	0
19	0	0	0
20	0	0	0
21	0	0	0
22+	0	0	0
			4.14

The data is shown in percentages, %

SECOND LEVEL MATRIX

	A(11)	2	2(12)	3	3(13)	4	4(14)	5	5(15)	6	6(16)	7	8	9	10	11	12	13	14	15	16	17	18	19	20	21	22+
A(11)	0	0	0	0	0.59	0	1.18	0	1.78	0	2.37	0	0	0	0	0	4.73	4.14	3.55	2.96	2.37	10.65	10.65	10.65	10.65	33.73	0
2	0	0	0	0	0	0	0.59	0	1.18	0.59	1.18	1.18	1.78	2.37	2.96	3.55	5.33	9.47	8.88	8.28	7.69	8.28	7.69	7.10	6.51	5.92	9.47
2(12)	0	0	0	0	0	0	0.59	0	1.18	0	1.78	0	0	0	0	0	2.37	6.51	5.92	5.33	4.73	12.43	12.43	12.43	12.43	12.43	9.47
3	0	0	0	0	0	0	0	0	0.59	0	1.18	0.59	1.18	1.78	2.37	2.96	4.73	5.33	9.47	8.88	8.28	8.88	8.28	7.69	7.10	6.51	14.20
3(13)	0	0	0	0	0	0	0	0	0.59	0	0	0	0	0	0	0	4.14	2.37	5.33	5.92	5.33	12.43	12.43	12.43	12.43	12.43	14.20
4	0	0	0	0	0	0	0	0	0	0	0	0	0.59	1.18	1.78	2.37	4.73	4.73	5.33	9.47	8.88	9.47	8.88	8.28	7.69	7.10	19.53
4(14)	0	0	0	0	0	0	0	0	0	0	0	0	0	0	0	0.59	1.18	1.78	2.37	6.51	5.92	12.43	12.43	12.43	12.43	12.43	19.53
5	0	0	0	0	0	0	0	0	0	0	0	0	0	0.59	1.18	1.78	3.55	4.14	4.73	5.33	9.47	9.47	9.47	8.88	8.28	7.69	25.44
5(15)	0	0	0	0	0	0	0	0	0	0	0	0	0	0	0	0	0.59	1.18	1.78	2.37	6.51	12.43	12.43	12.43	12.43	12.43	25.44
6	0	0	0	0	0	0	0	0	0	0	0	0	0	0	0.59	1.18	2.37	2.96	3.55	4.14	4.73	14.79	8.88	8.88	8.28	7.69	31.95
6(16)	0	0	0	0	0	0	0	0	0	0	0	0	0	0	0	0	0	0.59	1.18	1.78	2.37	12.43	12.43	12.43	12.43	12.43	31.95
7	0	0	0	0	0	0	0	0	0	0	0	0	0	0	0	0.59	1.78	2.37	2.96	3.55	4.14	35.50	12.43	6.51	6.51	5.92	17.75
8	0	0	0	0	0	0	0	0	0	0	0	0	0	0	0	0	1.18	1.78	2.37	2.96	3.55	11.83	34.91	11.83	5.92	5.92	17.75
9	0	0	0	0	0	0	0	0	0	0	0	0	0	0	0	0	0.59	1.18	1.78	2.37	2.96	11.24	11.24	34.32	11.24	5.33	17.75
10	0	0	0	0	0	0	0	0	0	0	0	0	0	0	0	0	0	0.59	1.18	1.78	2.37	10.65	10.65	10.65	33.73	10.65	17.75
11	0	0	0	0	0	0	0	0	0	0	0	0	0	0	0	0	0	0.59	1.18	1.78	2.37	10.65	10.65	10.65	10.65	33.73	17.75
12	0	0	0	0	0	0	0	0	0	0	0	0	0	0	0	0	0	0	0.59	1.18	1.78	10.06	10.06	10.06	10.06	10.06	46.15
13	0	0	0	0	0	0	0	0	0	0	0	0	0	0	0	0	0	0	0	0.59	1.18	9.47	9.47	9.47	9.47	9.47	50.89
14	0	0	0	0	0	0	0	0	0	0	0	0	0	0	0	0	0	0	0	0	0.59	8.88	8.88	8.88	8.88	8.88	55.03
15	0	0	0	0	0	0	0	0	0	0	0	0	0	0	0	0	0	0	0	0	0	8.28	8.28	8.28	8.28	8.28	58.58
16	0	0	0	0	0	0	0	0	0	0	0	0	0	0	0	0	0	0	0	0	0	7.69	7.69	7.69	7.69	7.69	61.54
17	0	0	0	0	0	0	0	0	0	0	0	0	0	0	0	0	0	0	0	0	0	100	0	0	0	0	0
18	0	0	0	0	0	0	0	0	0	0	0	0	0	0	0	0	0	0	0	0	0	0	100	0	0	0	0
19	0	0	0	0	0	0	0	0	0	0	0	0	0	0	0	0	0	0	0	0	0	0	0	100	0	0	0
20	0	0	0	0	0	0	0	0	0	0	0	0	0	0	0	0	0	0	0	0	0	0	0	0	100	0	0
21	0	0	0	0	0	0	0	0	0	0	0	0	0	0	0	0	0	0	0	0	0	0	0	0	0	100	0
22+	0	0	0	0	0	0	0	0	0	0	0	0	0	0	0	0	0	0	0	0	0	0	0	0	0	0	100

The data is shown in percentages, %

The second level matrix obtained, where every field will have the probability of going from one total to another with two extractions, will be multiplied, following this method, by the initial matrix in order to obtain the third level matrix; after a certain amount of multiplications we will have the final matrix, in which all the columns before 17 will contain zeros because the final totals will have "absorbed" all the other states:

FINAL MATRIX

	16 -	17	18	19	20	21	22 +
A(11)	0	13.08	13.08	13.08	13.08	36.16	11.53
2	0	13.98	13.49	12.97	12.40	11.80	35.36
2(12)	0	15.10	15.10	15.10	15.10	15.10	24.50
3	0	13.50	13.05	12.56	12.03	11.47	37.39
3(13)	0	14.55	14.55	14.55	14.55	14.55	27.25
4	0	13.05	12.59	12.14	11.65	11.12	39.45
4(14)	0	14.00	14.00	14.00	14.00	14.00	30
5	0	12.23	12.23	11.77	11.31	10.82	41.64
5(15)	0	13.46	13.46	13.46	13.46	13.46	32.72
6	0	16.54	10.63	10.63	10.17	9.72	42.32
6(16)	0	12.92	12.92	12.92	12.92	12.92	35.41
7	0	36.86	13.78	7.86	7.86	7.41	26.23
8	0	12.86	35.93	12.86	6.94	6.94	24.47
9	0	12.00	12.00	35.08	12.00	6.08	22.84
10	0	11.14	11.14	11.14	34.22	11.14	21.21
11	0	11.14	11.14	11.14	11.14	34.22	21.21
12	0	10.35	10.35	10.35	10.35	10.35	48.27
13	0	9.61	9.61	9.61	9.61	9.61	51.96
14	0	8.92	8.92	8.92	8.92	8.92	55.39
15	0	8.28	8.28	8.28	8.28	8.28	58.58
16	0	7.69	7.69	7.69	7.69	7.69	61.54
17	0	100	-	-	-	-	-
18	0	-	100	-	-	-	-
19	0	-	-	100	-	-	-
20	0	-	-	-	100	-	-
21	0	-	-	-	-	100	-
22 +	0	-	-	-	-	-	100

The data is shown in percentages, %

The chances of the dealer obtaining the various final totals starting from the possible initial states are highlighted in red; notice that they are identical to those previously calculated.

THE MATHS BEHIND THE GAME: THE PLAYER

Once the dealer's chances have been calculated, it is necessary to decide on the most advantageous move for the player in every game situation. Essentially there are three choices that must be made:
- Whether to hit or stand
- Whether to double down or not
- Whether to split or not
In each of these situations it is necessary to calculate the player's mathematical expectation for both choices in order to compare them and choose the most favourable option.

Hit/Stand:
Naturally this is the most common and most important choice, as in the majority of cases the player can neither split nor double down.
Given a game situation, first we must consider the probability that the player has of winning, losing or drawing if he decides to stand. These percentages are very simple to calculate, as they can be inferred by comparison with the dealer's chances, which have already been calculated and tabulated.
The next step is of course to calculate the probability that the player will win, lose or draw if he decides to hit. This calculation is slightly more complicated, as it is necessary to consider all the player's possible final results and compare them with those of the dealer, in order to then add up all the probabilities obtained.

For example, the player has hard 17 and the dealer 9.

The player stands, closes with 17, therefore:
- He wins if the dealer busts (22.84%)
- He draws if the dealer gets 17 (12.00%)
- He loses if the dealer gets 18, 19, 20 or 21 (65.16%)

The player hits, therefore:
- He wins if he draws a 4 and the dealer does not get 21 (1/13x93.92%=7.22%)
- He wins if he draws a 3 and the dealer does not get 20 or 21 (6.3%)
- He wins if he draws a 2 and the dealer does not get 19, 20 or 21 (3.6%)
- He wins if he draws an A and the dealer does not get 18, 19, 20 or 21 (2.68%)
- He draws if he draws a 4 and the dealer gets 21 (0.47%)
- He draws if he draws a 3 and the dealer gets 20 (0.92%)
- He draws if he draws a 2 and the dealer gets 19 (2.7%)
- He draws if he draws an A and the dealer gets 18 (0.92%)
- He loses if he draws a 5, 6, 7, 8, 9 or 10 (69.23%)

- He loses if he draws a 3 and the dealer gets 21 (0.47%)
- He loses if he draws a 2 and the dealer gets 20 or 21 (1.39%)
- He loses if he draws an A and the dealer gets 19, 20 or 21 (4.09%)

Overall, adding up the groups, we find that:
- He wins in 19.81% of cases
- He draws in 5.01% of cases
- He loses in 75.18% in cases

At this point it is necessary to compare the percentages obtained, to understand whether in the case examined it is effectively better to stand or hit. To do so we calculate the "mathematical expectation" of the player in both cases: the best choice will be the one with the greater mathematical expectation.

We will always bet 1 and not take draws into account, where the player recovers his bet without gain or loss.
If he stays in, out of 100 plays the player:
- Wins 22.84 bets
- Loses 65.16 bets

He will have therefore an imbalance of 65.16-22.84=42.32 betting units per 100 plays, which corresponds to an average loss of approximately 42 hundredths per hand. Let's say that if he stands, his mathematical expectation is -0.42.
If he hits, out of 100 plays, the player
- Wins 19.81 bets
- Loses 75.18 bets

He will have therefore an imbalance of 75.18-19.81=55.37 betting units per 100 plays, which corresponds to an average loss of approximately 55 hundredths per hand. Let's say that if he hits, his mathematical expectation is -0.55.

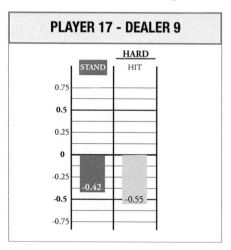

Let's try to fully grasp this.

It is an advantageous situation for the dealer either way, no matter what choice the player makes. The player has been "unlucky" and is at a disadvantage with this hand. But there is no doubt that it's better for the player to stand because losing an average of 42 hundredths is much better than losing 55. In other words, if the player hits, he "gives" the dealer 13 hundredths per hand and why on earth should he?

Similarly, let's go on to study the other cases.

Without expanding case by case, let us limit ourselves to tabulating, for every initial total greater than 10, all the possible states that a player might obtain by hitting.

Comparing each state and the respective percentages with the possible final states of the dealer, the player's odds of winning/losing/drawing are calculated for all cases in which he hits and this data is compared with the corresponding data should the player not hit, exactly as we saw in the example.

The sum of all the results will demonstrate the accuracy of the hit/stand table.

Of course the player may hit more than once, gradually reaching different states in succession. With a total of less than 11, hit in any case and this will always lead to one of the successive states.

TABLE OF OUTCOME PROBABILITIES
AFTER HITTING

INITIAL STATE	CARD DRAWN	FINAL STATE	PROBABILITY
20	A	21	7.69%
	2.3.4.5.6.7.8.9.10	22/+	92.31%
19	2	21	7.69%
	A	20	7.69%
	3.4.5.6.7.8.9.10	22/+	84.62%
18	3	21	7.69%
	2	20	7.69%
	A	19	7.69%
	4.5.6.7.8.9.10	22/+	76.92%
17	4	21	7.69%
	3	20	7.69%
	2	19	7.69%
	A	18	7.69%
	5.6.7.8.9.10	22/+	69.23%
16	5	21	7.69%
	4	20	7.69%
	3	19	7.69%
	2	18	7.69%
	A	17	7.69%
	6.7.8.9.10	22/+	61.64%
15	6	21	7.69%
	5	20	7.69%
	4	19	7.69%
	3	18	7.69%
	2	17	7.69%
	A	16	7.69%
	7.8.9.10	22/+	53.85%
14	7	21	7.69%
	6	20	7.69%
	5	19	7.69%
	4	18	7.69%
	3	17	7.69%
	2	16	7.69%
	A	15	7.69%
	8.9.10	22/+	46.15%

(continua)

INITIAL STATE	CARD DRAWN	FINAL STATE	PROBABILITY
13	8	21	7.69%
	7	20	7.69%
	6	19	7.69%
	5	18	7.69%
	4	17	7.69%
	3	16	7.69%
	2	15	7.69%
	A	14	7.69%
	9.10	22/+	38.46%
12	9	21	7.69%
	8	20	7.69%
	7	19	7.69%
	6	18	7.69%
	5	17	7.69%
	4	16	7.69%
	3	15	7.69%
	2	14	7.69%
	A	13	7.69%
	10	22/+	30.77%
11	10	21	30.77%
	9	20	7.69%
	8	19	7.69%
	7	18	7.69%
	6	17	7.69%
	5	16	7.69%
	4	15	7.69%
	3	14	7.69%
	2	13	7.69%
	A	12	7.69%

Soft hands

The probability of each game choice when the player has a "soft" total is calculated in exactly the same way as for hard hands. However, it should be considered that a "soft" hand has a different value to a hard hand, since there is no risk of going bust. The difference when doing the calculations lies in the fact that the successive totals obtained by the player for each draw are constructed differently. Let's see how:

STARTING TOTAL	CARD DRAWN	TOTAL OBTAINED	PROBABILITY
20 soft	A	21 soft	7.69%
	2	12	7.69%
	3	13	7.69%
	4	14	7.69%
	5	15	7.69%
	6	16	7.69%
	7	17	7.69%
	8	18	7.69%
	9	19	7.69%
	10	20	30.77%
19 soft	2	21 soft	7.69%
	A	20 soft	7.69%
	3	12	7.69%
	4	13	7.69%
	5	14	7.69%
	6	15	7.69%
	7	16	7.69%
	8	17	7.69%
	9	18	7.69%
	10	19	30.77%
18 soft	3	21 soft	7.69%
	2	20 soft	7.69%
	A	19 soft	7.69%
	4	12	7.69%
	5	13	7.69%
	6	14	7.69%
	7	15	7.69%
	8	16	7.69%
	9	17	7.69%
	10	18	30.77%

(continua)

STARTING TOTAL	CARD DRAWN	TOTAL OBTAINED	PROBABILITY
17 soft	4	21 soft	7.69%
	3	20 soft	7.69%
	2	19 soft	7.69%
	A	18 soft	7.69%
	5	12	7.69%
	6	13	7.69%
	7	14	7.69%
	8	15	7.69%
	9	16	7.69%
	10	17	30.77%
16 soft	5	21 soft	7.69%
	4	20 soft	7.69%
	3	19 soft	7.69%
	2	18 soft	7.69%
	A	17 soft	7.69%
	6	12	7.69%
	7	13	7.69%
	8	14	7.69%
	9	15	7.69%
	10	16	30.77%
15 soft	6	21 soft	7.69%
	5	20 soft	7.69%
	4	19 soft	7.69%
	3	18 soft	7.69%
	2	17 soft	7.69%
	A	16 soft	7.69%
	7	12	7.69%
	8	13	7.69%
	9	14	7.69%
	10	15	30.77%
14 soft	7	21 soft	7.69%
	6	20 soft	7.69%
	5	19 soft	7.69%
	4	18 soft	7.69%
	3	17 soft	7.69%
	2	16 soft	7.69%
	A	15 soft	7.69%
	8	12	7.69%
	9	13	7.69%
	10	14	30.77%

STARTING TOTAL	CARD DRAWN	TOTAL OBTAINED	PROBABILITY
13 soft	8	21 soft	7.69%
	7	20 soft	7.69%
	6	19 soft	7.69%
	5	18 soft	7.69%
	4	17 soft	7.69%
	3	16 soft	7.69%
	2	15 soft	7.69%
	A	14 soft	7.69%
	9	12	7.69%
	10	13	30.77%
12 soft	9	21 soft	7.69%
	8	20 soft	7.69%
	7	19 soft	7.69%
	6	18 soft	7.69%
	5	17 soft	7.69%
	4	16 soft	7.69%
	3	15 soft	7.69%
	2	14 soft	7.69%
	A	13 soft	7.69%
	10	12	30.77%

Double down

Let us look now at how to assess when it is advantageous for the player to double down in game situations where this is permitted. We must do a comparison similar to the one we saw in the case of Hit vs. Stand: the mathematical expectation relative to the most advantageous choice between standing and hitting will be compared to a new mathematical expectation relative to the case in which the player chooses to double down. The most advantageous choice for the player will of course be that with the greater mathematical expectation.

Through an example let's see how the odds are calculated when doubling down, remembering that if the player decides to double down, he receives one card and one card only.

The player has 9 against the dealer's 4.

The player does not double down and hits, therefore:

- He wins in 52.87% of cases
- He draws in 7.16% of cases
- He loses in 39.97% of cases

The player doubles down and receives a single card:

- He wins if he draws an A and the dealer does not get 20 or 21 (1/13x77.23%=5.94%)
- He wins if he draws a 10 and the dealer does not get 19, 20 or 21 (20.03%)
- He wins if he draws a 9 and the dealer does not get 18, 19, 20 or 21 (4.04%)
- He wins if he draws an 8, 7, 6, 5, 4, 3 or 2 and the dealer goes bust (21.24%)
- He draws if he draws an A and the dealer gets 20 (0.90%)
- He draws if he draws a 10 and the dealer gets 19 (3.73%)
- He draws if he draws a 9 and the dealer gets 18 (0.97%)
- He draws if he draws an 8 and the dealer gets 17 (1.00%)
- He loses if he draws an A and the dealer gets 21 (0.86%)
- He loses if he draws a 10 and the dealer gets 20 or 21 (7.01%)
- He loses if he draws a 9 and the dealer gets 19, 20 or 21 (2.69%)
- He loses if he draws an 8 and the dealer gets 18, 19, 20 or 21 (3.65%)
- He loses if he draws a 2, 3, 4, 5, 6 or 7 and the dealer does not go bust (27.95%)

Overall, adding up by groups, we find that:

- He wins in 51.25% of cases
- He draws in 6.60% of cases
- He loses in 42.15% of cases

At this point, we compare the mathematical expectation of the two cases.

If he does not double down, always assuming the bet is 1 and not considering a draw, out of 100 plays the player:

- Wins 52.87 bets
- Loses 39.97 bets

He will have therefore an imbalance of 52.87-39.97=12.9 betting units for every 100 plays, in other words an average gain of approximately 13 hundredths per hand. Let's say that if he does not double down his mathematical expectation is 0.13.

If he doubles down we must consider betting 2 units and no longer 1, so for 100 plays the player:

• Wins 2x51.25 bets
• Loses 2x42.15 bets

Therefore he will have an imbalance of 102.49-84.3=18.19 betting units for every 100 plays, in other words, an average gain of approximately 18 hundredths. If he doubles down, his mathematical expectation is 0.18.

We have before us a favourable situation for the player, as his mathematical expectation is advantageous regardless of his choice; however, if he decides to double down he is guaranteed an average gain of 18 hundredths compared to an average gain of 13 hundredths if he does not double down. Why should he let those 5 hundredths go?

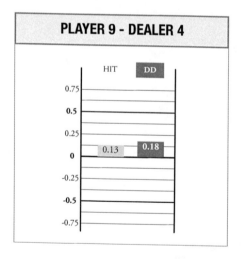

Split

The other fundamental choice a player has to make is deciding whether to split or not when he receives two cards of equal value. In this case the mathematical expectation relative to the most advantageous choice between standing, hitting or doubling will be compared to that relative to the decision to split the pair. To calculate this latter we must bear in mind that, when the player decides to split a pair into two separate hands, he may win or lose them both, he may win one and lose the other, win one and draw the other, or lose one and draw the other. As usual, let us see the mechanisms of the calculation with an example.

The player has a pair of 5's, against the dealer's 9.

The player does not split, but doubles down, since we know that with 10 against 9 it is best to double down, we find that:

• He wins in 49.26% of cases
• He draws 8.70% of cases
• He loses in 42.04% of cases

The player splits.

In this case we calculate the probability starting from a total of 5. The system is the same as that used in the paragraph concerning hit/stand, except that it starts from a situation in which the player has only one card and therefore automatically hits (at least for the second card), in order to reach a value between 11 and 21, just as in the *Table of outcome probabilities after hitting* table.

Adding all the single probabilities of all the possible situations that may arise (we'll spare you the calculation, quite mechanical) we find that each separate hand with 5:

• Wins in 32.14% of cases
• Draws in 9.07% of cases
• Loses in 58.80% of cases

But after the split there are two hands with 5 and the outcomes may occur in various ways:

• **Both hands win**
(Two bets are won) in 32.14%x32.14%=10.33% of cases
• **One hand wins and one draws**
(One bet is won) in (32.14%x9.07%)x2=5.83% of cases
• **One hand wins and one loses**
(Balanced) in (32.14%x58.80%)x2=37.79% of cases
• **Both hands draw**
(Balanced) in 9.07%x9.07%=0.82% of cases
• **One hand draws and one loses**
(One bet is lost) in (9.07%x58.80%)x2=10.66% of cases

• Both hands lose

(Two bets are lost) in 58.80%x58.80%=34.57% of cases

Now all that remains is to calculate the two mathematical expectations and compare them. If he does not split the player doubles down, therefore he bets two units. Out of 100 plays:
• He wins 2x49.26 bets
• He loses 2x42.04 bets

Therefore he will have an imbalance of 98.51-84.08=14.43 betting points each 100 plays, in other words, an average gain of 14 hundredths a hand. If he does not split the pair his mathematical expectation is 0.14.

If instead he decides to split, out of 100 plays, the player:
• Wins 2x10.33+1x5.83=26.48 bets
• Loses 2x34.57+1x10.66=79.8 bets

Therefore he will have an imbalance of 26.48-79.8=-53.32 betting units every 100 plays, he will therefore have an average loss of approximately 53 hundredths. His mathematical expectation in this case is -0.53.

In this situation it is clear that the player should not split the pair of 5's because if he does so his mathematical expectation not only decreases but becomes negative, when he could remain on positive ground.

He would lose an average of 0.14-(-053) =0.67 hundredths a play!

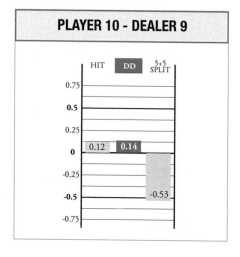

	2	3	4	5	6	7	8	9	10	A
4	-0.11 hit	-0.08 hit	-0.05 hit	-0.01 hit	0.01 hit	-0.09 hit	-0.16 hit	-0.24 hit	-0.34 hit	-0.48 hit
5	-0.13 hit	-0.10 hit	-0.06 hit	-0.02 hit	-0.01 hit	-0.12 hit	-0.19 hit	-0.27 hit	-0.37 hit	-0.50 hit
6	-0.14 hit	-0.11 hit	-0.07 hit	-0.03 hit	-0.01 hit	-0.15 hit	-0.22 hit	-0.29 hit	-0.39 hit	-0.52 hit
7	-0.11 hit	-0.08 hit	-0.04 hit	-0.01 hit	0.03 hit	-0.07 hit	-0.21 hit	-0.29 hit	-0.37 hit	-0.52 hit
8	-0.02 hit	0.01 hit	0.04 hit	0.07 hit	0.11 hit	0.08 hit	-0.06 hit	-0.21 hit	-0.31 hit	-0.44 hit
9	0.07 hit	0.12 DD	0.18 DD	0.24 DD	0.32 DD	0.17 hit	0.10 hit	-0.05 hit	-0.22 hit	-0.35 hit
10	0.36 DD	0.41 DD	0.46 DD	0.51 DD	0.58 DD	0.39 DD	0.29 DD	0.14 DD	-0.06 hit	-0.25 hit
11	0.47 DD	0.52 DD	0.57 DD	0.61 DD	0.67 DD	0.46 DD	0.35 DD	0.23 DD	0.03 hit	-0.21 hit
12	-0.25 hit	-0.23 hit	-0.21 stand	-0.17 stand	-0.15 stand	-0.21 hit	-0.27 hit	-0.34 hit	-0.43 hit	-0.55 hit
13	-0.29 stand	-0.25 stand	-0.21 stand	-0.17 stand	-0.15 stand	-0.27 hit	-0.32 hit	-0.39 hit	-0.47 hit	-0.58 hit
14	-0.29 stand	-0.25 stand	-0.21 stand	-0.17 stand	-0.15 stand	-0.32 hit	-0.37 hit	-0.43 hit	-0.51 hit	-0.61 hit
15	-0.29 stand	-0.25 stand	-0.21 stand	-0.17 stand	-0.15 stand	-0.37 hit	-0.42 hit	-0.47 hit	-0.54 hit	-0.64 hit
16	-0.29 stand	-0.25 stand	-0.21 stand	-0.17 stand	-0.15 stand	-0.41 hit	-0.46 hit	-0.51 hit	-0.58 hit	-0.67 hit
17	-0.15 stand	-0.12 stand	-0.08 stand	-0.04 stand	0.01 stand	-0.11 stand	-0.38 stand	-0.42 stand	-0.46 stand	-0.46 stand
18	0.12 stand	0.15 stand	0.18 stand	0.20 stand	0.28 stand	0.40 stand	0.11 stand	-0.18 stand	-0.24 stand	-0.38 stand
19	0.39 stand	0.40 stand	0.42 stand	0.44 stand	0.50 stand	0.62 stand	0.59 stand	0.29 stand	-0.02 stand	-0.12 stand
20	0.64 stand	0.65 stand	0.66 stand	0.67 stand	0.70 stand	0.77 stand	0.79 stand	0.76 stand	0.43 stand	0.15 stand
A+2	0.05 hit	0.08 hit	0.10 hit	0.13 DD	0.18 DD	0.12 hit	0.05 hit	-0.04 hit	-0.17 hit	-0.35 hit
A+3	0.02 hit	0.05 hit	0.08 hit	0.12 DD	0.18 DD	0.08 hit	0.01 hit	-0.08 hit	-0.21 hit	-0.37 hit
A+4	0 hit	0.03 hit	0.06 DD	0.13 DD	0.18 DD	0.04 hit	-0.03 hit	-0.11 hit	-0.24 hit	-0.40 hit
A+5	-0.02 hit	0.01 hit	0.06 DD	0.13 DD	0.18 DD	0 hit	-0.07 hit	-0.15 hit	-0.27 hit	-0.42 hit
A+6	0 hit	0.05 DD	0.12 DD	0.18 DD	0.26 DD	0.05 hit	-0.07 hit	-0.15 hit	-0.26 hit	-0.43 hit
A+7	0.12 stand	0.18 DD	0.24 DD	0.30 DD	0.38 DD	0.40 stand	0.11 stand	-0.10 hit	-0.21 hit	-0.37 hit
A+8	0.39 stand	0.40 stand	0.42 stand	0.44 stand	0.50 stand	0.62 stand	0.59 stand	0.29 stand	-0.02 stand	-0.12 stand
A+9	0.64 stand	0.65 stand	0.66 stand	0.67 stand	0.70 stand	0.77 stand	0.79 stand	0.76 stand	0.43 stand	0.15 stand
2+2	-0.11 hit	-0.08 hit	-0.04 split	0.03 split	0.08 split	-0.05 split	-0.16 hit	-0.24 hit	-0.34 hit	-0.48 hit
3+3	-0.14 hit	-0.11 hit	-0.07 split	0 split	0.05 split	-0.11 split	-0.22 hit	-0.29 hit	-0.39 hit	-0.52 hit
4+4	-0.02 hit	0.01 hit	0.04 hit	0.07 hit	0.11 hit	0.08 hit	-0.06 hit	-0.21 hit	-0.31 hit	-0.44 hit
5+5	0.36 DD	0.41 DD	0.46 DD	0.51 DD	0.58 DD	0.39 DD	0.29 DD	0.14 DD	-0.06 hit	-0.25 hit
6+6	-0.25 hit	-0.21 split	-0.14 split	-0.07 split	-0.03 split	-0.21 hit	-0.27 hit	-0.34 hit	-0.43 hit	-0.55 hit
7+7	-0.22 split	-0.15 split	-0.09 split	-0.01 split	0.06 split	-0.14 split	-0.37 hit	-0.43 hit	-0.51 hit	-0.61 hit
8+8	-0.04 split	0.02 split	0.08 split	0.14 split	0.23 split	0.16 split	-0.12 split	-0.42 split	-0.58 hit	-0.67 hit
9+9	0.15 split	0.20 split	0.26 split	0.32 split	0.39 split	0.40 stand	0.20 split	-0.10 split	-0.24 stand	-0.38 stand
10+10	0.64 stand	0.65 stand	0.66 stand	0.67 stand	0.70 stand	0.77 stand	0.79 stand	0.76 stand	0.43 stand	0.15 stand
A+A	0.47 split	0.52 split	0.57 split	0.61 split	0.67 split	0.46 split	0.35 split	0.23 split	0.06 split	-0.32 hit

We close this chapter with the general table once more, showing all the explicit cases, and above all, showing the mathematical expectation corresponding to the best decision for every single situation.

As well as a summary of all the decisions to be made, in this way the player can always be sure whether or not he finds himself in an advantageous, or not so advantageous, position.

The red zones indicate the player's advantage and the darker the red, the more he is at an advantage.

The grey zones indicate the player's disadvantage and the darker the grey, the more he is at a disadvantage.

HOW TO PLAY AND WHY

Blackjack
She's a hell of a thrill
Blackjack
She's makin' a kill
Fever runnin' high
Got aces in my eyes

Blackjack (album Runnin' Wild, 2007)
Airbourn

ANALYSIS OF EVERY GAME SITUATION

Now we've seen the "tables" all that remains is to follow them in order to make the best possible decision in every game situation. The combination of these tables defines the so-called "basic strategy".

In the section on mathematics we also showed how these details are calculated, meaning sceptics can verify the how and why of every decision suggested.

In this chapter we will look at all the individual situations that may happen at the table one by one and compare the mathematical expectations of all the options that may arise from them, calculated with the methods described in the preceding chapters. It is assessed case by case to what extent a correct decision is better than an incorrect one, in other words: what is the cost of a bad decision.

There are situations which are favourable to the dealer either way, where it is necessary to choose the lesser loss, others are instead favourable to the player either way and the greater gain must be chosen.

We will also see how options reserved for the player (double down and split) can lead to extremely advantageous situations for the player if properly exploited. A good player will in essence make the decision that corresponds to the best mathematic expectation, the decision that on average, if playing infinitely, will win the most... or lose the least.

As a first example let's look at *player 15 - dealer 9*:

player	dealer	hand	decision	mathematical expectation	loss
15	9	hard	stand	-0.54	0.07
			hit	-0.47	-
		soft	stand	-0.54	0.43
			hit	-0.11	-

The options are stand or hit, be it a hard or soft hand. If the player stands, the mathematical expectation is -0.54, meaning that on average he would lose 54 hundredths of the bet every hand (meaning 54 bets every 100 hands).

The outcome of the decision to hit varies depending whether the hand is hard (e.g. 5+3+7) or soft (e.g. A+4).

If the player hits with a hard hand, his mathematical expectation becomes -0.47, meaning an average loss of 47 hundredths of the bet per hand, which is still better than a loss of 54 had he decided to stand. So standing is like handing over 7 hundredths to the dealer, the equivalent of 7 bets every 100 hands. But why should a player hand this over? The player must not stand, full stop. If the player has a soft hand and hits, his situation improves decidedly as the mathematical expectation rises to -0.11, meaning "only" losing an average of 11 hundredths of the bet per hand. In this case the difference is greater; standing with a soft hand would cost 43 hundredths of the bet per hand.

In both cases hitting improves the mathematical expectation, therefore the right choice is always to hit, be it with a soft hand or a hard hand.

This same situation is best viewed with a block diagram, where it becomes immediately clear, with the best decisions highlighted in red.

Now let us look at an example where the player's choice varies depending whether his total is with a hard or soft hand:

player 13 - dealer 3

player	dealer	hand	decision	mathematical expectation	loss
13	5	hard	stand	-0.17	-
			hit	-0.26	0.09
		soft	stand	-0.17	0.30
			hit	0.13	-

In this case too, the only options are to stand or hit.

Standing gives a mathematical expectation of -0.17, meaning a loss of 17 hundredths of the bet a hand on average (17 bets lost every 100 hands).

Hitting instead leads to different results depending whether the player's hand is hard or soft.

If the player has a hard hand (e.g. 10+3) and decides to hit rather than stand, his mathematical expectation becomes -0.26, increasing his average loss to 26 hundredths of the bet a hand. Hitting costs 9 hundredths a hand. The player must stand.

If the player has a soft hand instead, hitting would put him in a more favourable position than the dealer, arriving at an average gain of 13 hundredths of the bet per hand. The decision is turned on its head then, better to hit and gain 13 hundredths than stand and lose 17. Standing would be like giving 30 hundredths to the dealer. The player must hit.

We will also view this case with a block diagram. If it's a hard hand it's best to stand, if it's soft, hit.

Finally we will examine a more complicated case, analysing all the possible options: *player 18 - dealer 8*

player	dealer	hand	decision	mathematical expectation	loss
18	8	hard	stand	0.11	-
			hit	-0.59	0.70
		9+9	stand	0.11	0.09
			split	0.20	-
		soft	stand	0.11	
			hit	0.04	0.07
		soft A+7	DD	-0.03	0.14

The choice is not always between standing and hitting only, in some specific cases we will have to decide whether to split (with an initial 9+9) and whether to double down (with an initial A+7).

From the table we can see that the choice to stand leads to an average gain of 11 hundredths per hand, while hitting leads to a worse outcome. If the player hits with a hard hand, the mathematical expectation becomes decidedly negative (-0.59), this decision leads to an average cost of 70 hundredths per hand (0.11+0.59).
If the player stands with a soft hand, he remains in positive territory (+0.04), but the average gain decreases by 7 hundredths per hand.
In both cases the player must stand.

If the player's 18 is made up of 9+9, the possibility of splitting comes into play. If this option is chosen, the average gain increases in comparison to the decision to stand, from 0.11 to 0.20. In this case the player should split the pair, why give up those 9 hundredths per hand?
With an initial Ace and 7 on the other hand, we can consider doubling down, but doubling down would be an error because this decision leads to a decrease in mathematical expectation to -0.03, at a cost of 14 hundredths a hand in comparison with the decision to stand.

In conclusion, with 18 against 9, the player should always stand, unless he started with 9+9, in which case he should split.

This data can be seen more clearly in a block diagram.

We will continue this chapter by considering all the possible totals of the player

PLAYER 18 - DEALER 8

		HARD		SOFT	
	STAND	HIT	9+9 SPLIT	HIT	A+7 DD

Values shown: STAND 0.11, 9+9 SPLIT 0.20, HIT (hard) -0.59, HIT (soft) 0.04, A+7 DD -0.03

and the dealer. And for each situation we will show a diagram with the mathematical expectation of every single possible option.

For every player total there will also be a summarising table that (as well as tables of decisions and mathematical expectations) will also sum up the odds of winning, drawing or losing in every situation, for every choice.

You will notice that in the event of splits, the percentages are more complex as the winnings may be 2 totals (if both hands are won) or one total (if one is won and one is drawn), and the same goes for losses.

THE PLAYER HAS 20

When the player has a 20 in hand, he must never hit, under any circumstances. It is a game situation which is favourable to him either way, no matter what the dealer's up card may be, the player's mathematical expectation is positive. If he were to hit, he would only have 1 chance in 13 of increasing his total.

That the player must stand is clear from the mathematical data.

If he stands, his mathematical expectation is between +0.64 and 0.79 when the dealer has between 2 and 9 and is still positive even if the dealer has a 10 or an Ace. Hitting with a hard hand would be a sort of mathematical catastrophe, with an expectation between -0.85 and -0.90, almost a certain loss.

Hitting with a soft hand would not be as catastrophic, but would be a mistake nevertheless, because the expectation – though sometimes positive – is always inferior to the option of standing.

The great difference between hard and soft hands is owed to the fact that you can never go bust with a soft hand, certainly you can worsen your situation (meaning obtaining a total lesser than that with which you started), but not go bust.

If the player has two initial cards with a value of 10, theoretically he can split; that is, divide the cards and play two separate hands. Mathematics tells us that we must never do so, no matter what the dealer's up card.

An incorrect choice can in some cases lead to a very limited error (against a dealer's 6 for example, the average win is 0.69 if you split and 0.70 if not), but if the dealer starts with a 10 or an Ace the player would find himself with a negative expectation.

In order to calculate the mathematical probability in the case of splitting 10's, not only the probability of winning, losing or drawing was taken into consideration, but also the possibility of getting blackjack by drawing an Ace.

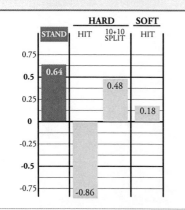

PLAYER 20 - DEALER 2

HARD | SOFT

STAND | HIT | 10+10 SPLIT | HIT

- 0.64 (STAND)
- 0.48 (10+10 SPLIT)
- 0.18 (SOFT HIT)
- -0.86 (HARD HIT)

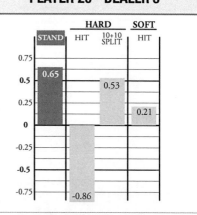

PLAYER 20 - DEALER 3

HARD | SOFT

STAND | HIT | 10+10 SPLIT | HIT

- 0.65 (STAND)
- 0.53 (10+10 SPLIT)
- 0.21 (SOFT HIT)
- -0.86 (HARD HIT)

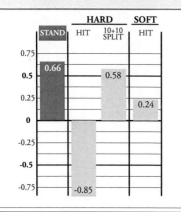

PLAYER 20 - DEALER 4

HARD | SOFT

STAND | HIT | 10+10 SPLIT | HIT

- 0.66 (STAND)
- 0.58 (10+10 SPLIT)
- 0.24 (SOFT HIT)
- -0.85 (HARD HIT)

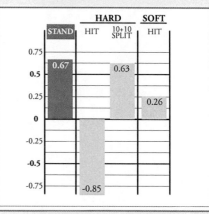

PLAYER 20 - DEALER 5

HARD | SOFT

STAND | HIT | 10+10 SPLIT | HIT

- 0.67 (STAND)
- 0.63 (10+10 SPLIT)
- 0.26 (SOFT HIT)
- -0.85 (HARD HIT)

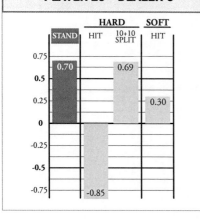

PLAYER 20 - DEALER 6

HARD | SOFT

STAND | HIT | 10+10 SPLIT | HIT

- 0.70 (STAND)
- 0.69 (10+10 SPLIT)
- 0.30 (SOFT HIT)
- -0.85 (HARD HIT)

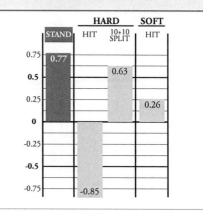

PLAYER 20 - DEALER 7

HARD | SOFT

STAND | HIT | 10+10 SPLIT | HIT

- 0.77 (STAND)
- 0.63 (10+10 SPLIT)
- 0.26 (SOFT HIT)
- -0.85 (HARD HIT)

PLAYER 20 - DEALER 8

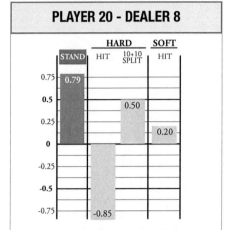

PLAYER 20 - DEALER 9

PLAYER 20 - DEALER 10

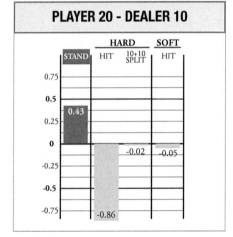

PLAYER 20 - DEALER A

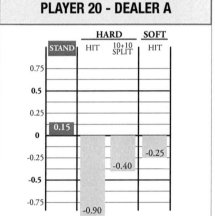

player	dealer	hand	decision	expectation[1]	loss[2]	wins[3]	draws[3]	loses[3]
20	2		stand	0.64	-	75.80	12.40	11.80
		hard	hit	-0.86	1.50	6.78	0.91	92.31
		10+10	split	0.48	0.16	35.72(x2)+8.74(x1)	44.48	13.52(x2)+5.37(x1)
		soft	hit	0.18	0.46	55.02	8.22	36.77
	3		stand	0.65	-	76.47	12.03	11.50
		hard	hit	-0.86	1.51	6.81	0.88	92.31
		10+10	split	0.53	0.12	37.26(x2)+8.64(x1)	44.10	12.75(x2)+5.06(x1)
		soft	hit	0.21	0.44	57.21	7.08	35.71
	4		stand	0.66	-	77.23	11.65	11.12
		hard	hit	-0.85	1.51	6.84	0.86	92.31
		10+10	split	0.58	0.08	39.13(x2)+8.12(x1)	43.96	12.11(x2)+4.52(x1)
		soft	hit	0.24	0.42	58.71	6.49	34.80
	5		stand	0.67	-	77.86	11.31	10.82
		hard	hit	-0.85	1.52	6.86	0.83	92.31
		10+10	split	0.63	0.04	40.89(x2)+8.02(x1)	43.41	11.31(x2)+4.22(x1)
		soft	hit	0.26	0.41	60.10	6.27	33.64
	6		stand	0.70	-	80.11	10.17	9.72
		hard	hit	-0.85	1.55	6.94	0.75	92.31
		10+10	split	0.69	0.01	43.02(x2)+7.92(x1)	42.63	10.38(x2)+3.89(x1)
		soft	hit	0.30	0.40	61.74	6.04	32.22
	7		stand	0.77	-	84.73	7.86	7.41
		hard	hit	-0.85	1.62	7.12	0.57	92.31
		10+10	split	0.63	0.14	38.74(x2)+11.78(x1)	40.90	10.33(x2)+6.08(x1)
		soft	hit	0.26	0.51	58.40	9.46	32.14
	8		stand	0.79	-	86.12	6.94	6.94
		hard	hit	-0.85	1.64	7.16	0.53	92.31
		10+10	split	0.50	0.29	35.13(x2)+11.24(x1)	42.50	12.32(x2)+6.66(x1)
		soft	hit	0.20	0.59	54.89	10.02	35.09
	9		stand	0.76	-	81.92	12.00	6.08
		hard	hit	-0.85	1.61	7.22	0.47	92.31
		10+10	split	0.33	0.43	29.66(x2)+11.87(x1)	43.11	14.82(x2)+8.39(x1)
		soft	hit	0.12	0.64	50.14	11.37	38.49
	10		stand	0.43	-	54.64	34.22	11.14
		hard	hit	-0.86	1.29	6.84	0.27	92.90
		10+10	split	-0.02	0.45	18.69(x2)+13.96(x1)	40.80	19.52(x2)+14.26(x1)
		soft	hit	-0.05	0.48	39.41	15.82	44.77
	A		stand	0.15	-	50.75	13.08	36.15
		hard	hit	-0.90	1.05	4.91	0.41	94.67
		10+10	split	-0.40	0.55	12.81(x2)+8.16(x1)	41.01	30.78(x2)+12.65(x1)
		soft	hit	-0.25	0.40	32.71	9.45	57.84

[1] *Mathematical expectation.*
[2] *Average cost of an incorrect decision, in bets lost per hand.*
[3] *Data in percentages, %.*

THE PLAYER HAS 19

With a total of 19 the player must always stand, whether with a hard or soft hand. The mathematical expectation when standing is positive when the dealer has between 2 and 9 (between +0.29 and +0.62); if however the dealer's first card is a 10 or an Ace, the player is at a disadvantage, although standing remains the correct choice.

Against the dealer's Ace the player will have an expected average loss of 12 bets out of 100 hands played; but this casts no doubts on the game tactic, as hitting would on average lose much more (81 bets per 100 hands)

.

PLAYER 19 - DEALER 2

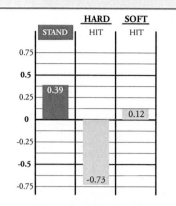

PLAYER 19 - DEALER 3

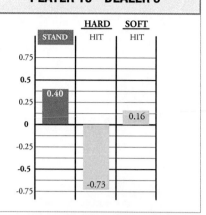

PLAYER 19 - DEALER 4

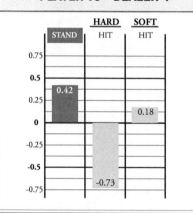

PLAYER 19 - DEALER 5

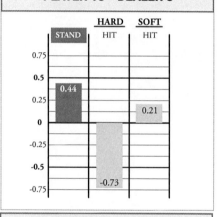

PLAYER 19 - DEALER 6

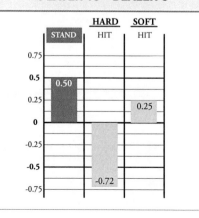

PLAYER 19 - DEALER 7

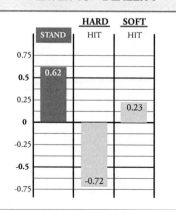

PLAYER 19 - DEALER 8

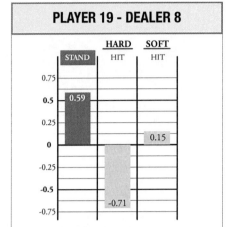

PLAYER 19 - DEALER 9

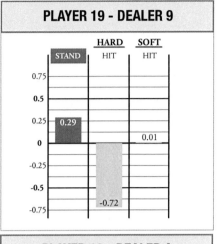

PLAYER 19 - DEALER 10

PLAYER 19 - DEALER A

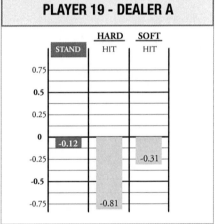

player	dealer	hand	decision	expectation[1]	loss[2]	wins[3]	draws[3]	loses[3]
19	2		stand	0.39	-	62.83	12.97	24.20
		hard	hit	-0.73	1.12	12.62	1.86	85.52
		soft	hit	0.12	0.27	52.02	8.35	39.63
	3		stand	0.40	-	63.92	12.56	23.53
		hard	hit	-0.73	1.13	12.69	1.81	85.50
		soft	hit	0.16	0.24	54.30	7.20	38.49
	4		stand	0.42	-	65.09	12.14	22.77
		hard	hit	-0.73	1.15	12.78	1.75	85.47
		soft	hit	0.18	0.24	55.91	6.60	37.49
	5		stand	0.44	-	66.09	11.77	22.14
		hard	hit	-0.73	1.17	12.85	1.70	85.45
		soft	hit	0.21	0.23	57.38	6.37	36.25
	6		stand	0.50	-	69.49	10.63	19.89
		hard	hit	-0.72	1.22	13.11	1.53	85.36
		soft	hit	0.25	0.25	59.29	6.14	34.57
	7		stand	0.62	-	76.87	7.86	15.27
		hard	hit	-0.72	1.34	13.64	1.17	85.19
		soft	hit	0.23	0.39	56.58	9.46	33.95
	8		stand	0.59	-	73.26	12.86	13.88
		hard	hit	-0.71	1.30	13.78	1.07	85.15
		soft	hit	0.15	0.44	51.92	11.38	36.70
	9		stand	0.29	-	46.84	35.08	18.08
		hard	hit	-0.72	1.01	13.53	1.39	85.08
		soft	hit	0.01	0.28	42.05	16.69	41.26
	10		stand	-0.02	-	43.50	11.14	45.36
		hard	hit	-0.75	0.73	11.04	2.90	86.06
		soft	hit	-0.16	0.14	36.84	10.49	52.67
	A		stand	-0.12	-	37.68	13.08	49.25
		hard	hit	-0.81	0.69	8.82	1.42	89.76
		soft	hit	-0.31	0.19	29.69	9.45	60.86

[1] *Mathematical expectation.*
[2] *Average cost of an incorrect decision, in bets lost per hand.*
[3] *Data in percentages, %.*

THE PLAYER HAS 18

> **STAND WITH HARD HAND**
> **SPLIT WITH 9-9 AGAINST 2, 3, 4, 5, 6, 8, 9**
> **HIT WITH SOFT HAND AGAINST 9, 10, A**
> **DOUBLE DOWN WITH A-7 AGAINST 3, 4, 5, 6**

A total of 18 is very good, in fact, in the majority of cases, the mathematical expectation is positive with the right decision.

We can see from the data shown below that with a hard total the correct choice is to stand. The expected winnings start from +0.12 (against the dealer's 2) and grow to +0.40 (against a 7); they then decrease to 0.11 when the dealer has 8, as the chances of drawing increase (the dealer reaches 18 with any 10) and finally the expected win becomes negative if the dealer has a 9, 10 or Ace, as in these cases the dealer has a good chance of closing with 19, 20 or 21.

Things change with a soft 18, the difference between the two mathematical expectations is very low and sometimes it is advantageous to hit.

If the dealer has a card between 2 and 8 the choice to stand is correct, the most favourable situation is when the dealer has a 7 as there is a high chance that he will reach 17, a total that forces him to stand and lose.

The situation is reversed if the dealer has a 9, 10 or an Ace, the player finds himself at a disadvantage and the correct choice is to hit in order to minimise the loss.

A+7

In some casinos, as mentioned above, it is permitted to double down whatever the value of the two initial cards. This may be advantageous in various situations with hard totals of 9, 10 and 11 and also with some soft totals.

If the first two cards are A+8 or A+9 the player should never double down, as he already has a good total in hand with little chance of improving it. With A+7 though, it begins to be an option worth considering, if the dealer has 3, 4, 5, or 6, the player should double down! In other cases the normal strategy for soft 18 should be followed.

Finally, if the dealer has a 9, 10 or an Ace he is at an advantage and so doubling down in this case would be madness… we would be doubling our losses.

9+9

If the dealer's up card is between 2 and 8, the hand is in the player's favour and splitting increases the expected earnings by approximately 10 hundredths per bet. The only exception is against the dealer's 7, which we know to be a particularly advantageous situation for the player, in this case by dividing the pair of nines, he would lose part of the advantage (from +0.40 to +0.34).

In circumstances that are unfavourable to the player, we observe that against a 9 it is best to split to decrease the loss, while against a 10 or an Ace we must absolutely not do so because we would double our disadvantage.

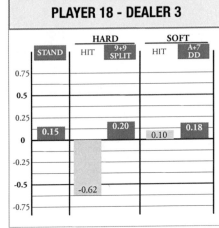

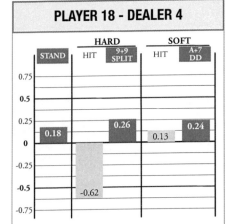

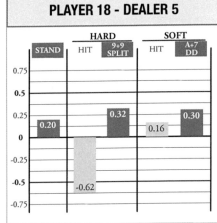

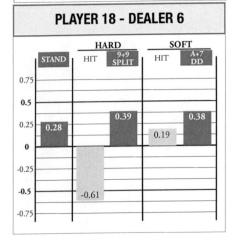

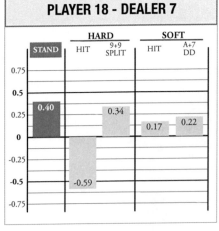

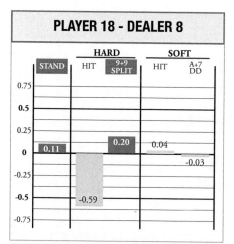

PLAYER 18 - DEALER 8

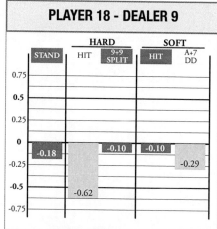

PLAYER 18 - DEALER 9

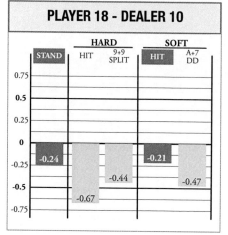

PLAYER 18 - DEALER 10

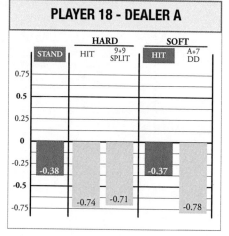

PLAYER 18 - DEALER A

player	dealer	hand	decision	expectation[1]	loss[2]	wins[3]	draws[3]	loses[3]
18	2	hard	stand	0.12	-	49.34	13.49	37.17
			hit	-0.60	0.72	18.36	2.86	78.78
		9+9	stand	0.12	0.03	49.34	13.49	37.17
			split	0.15	-	24.70(x2)+8.01(x1)	42.64	17.85(x2)+6.81(x1)
		soft	stand	0.12	-	49.34	13.49	37.17
			hit	0.06	0.06	48.91	8.47	42.62
		A+7	DD	0.12	0.00	48.95	8.09	42.97
	3	hard	stand	0.15	-	50.87	13.05	36.08
			hit	-0.62	0.77	17.61	2.77	79.61
		9+9	stand	0.15	0.05	50.87	13.05	36.08
			split	0.20	-	26.16(x2)+7.98(x1)	42.59	16.84(x2)+6.40(x1)
		soft	stand	0.15	-	50.87	13.05	36.08
			hit	0.10	0.05	51.30	7.31	41.39
		A+7	stand	0.15	0.03	50.87	13.05	36.08
			DD	0.18	-	50.51	7.83	41.67
	4	hard	stand	0.18	-	52.50	12.59	34.91
			hit	-0.62	0.80	17.78	2.69	79.53
		9+9	stand	0.18	0.08	52.50	12.59	34.91
			split	0.26	-	27.95(x2)+7.57(x1)	42.78	15.98(x2)+5.72(x1)
		soft	stand	0.18	-	52.50	12.59	34.91
			hit	0.13	0.05	53.00	6.71	40.29
		A+7	DD	0.24	-	52.14	7.56	40.29
	5	hard	stand	0.20	-	53.87	12.23	33.91
			hit	-0.62	0.82	17.93	2.61	79.46
		9+9	stand	0.20	0.12	53.87	12.23	33.91
			split	0.32	-	29.64(x2)+7.52(x1)	42.56	14.93(x2)+5.34(x1)
		soft	stand	0.20	-	53.87	12.23	33.91
			hit	0.16	0.04	54.56	6.48	38.96
		A+7	DD	0.30	-	53.73	7.31	38.96
	6	hard	stand	0.28	-	58.86	10.63	30.51
			hit	-0.61	0.89	18.45	2.35	79.20
		9+9	stand	0.28	0.11	58.86	10.63	30.51
			split	0.39	-	31.89(x2)+7.52(x1)	42.09	13.59(x2)+4.91(x1)
		soft	stand	0.28	-	58.86	10.63	30.51
			hit	0.19	0.09	56.13	6.85	37.02
		A+7	DD	0.38	-	56.09	6.89	37.02
	7	hard	stand	0.40	-	63.09	13.78	23.13
			hit	-0.59	0.99	19.55	1.78	78.67
		9+9	split	0.34	0.06	28.60(x2)+10.94(x1)	39.86	13.17(x2)+7.42(x1)
		soft	stand	0.40	-	63.09	13.78	23.13
			hit	0.17	0.23	52.83	11.40	35.77
		A+7	DD	0.22	0.18	51.07	8.85	40.07

player	dealer	hand	decision	expectation[1]	loss[2]	wins[3]	draws[3]	loses[3]
18	8	hard	stand	0.11	-	37.33	35.93	26.74
			hit	-0.59	0.70	19.42	2.06	78.52
		9+9	stand	0.11	0.09	37.33	35.93	26.74
			split	0.20	-	24.12(x2)+11.41(x1)	39.92	15.42(x2)+9.13(x1)
		soft	stand	0.11	-	37.33	35.93	26.74
			hit	0.04	0.07	43.63	16.71	39.66
		A+7	DD	-0.03	0.14	42.20	14.10	43.70
	9	hard	stand	-0.18	-	34.84	12.00	53.16
			hit	-0.62	0.44	17.13	4.09	78.78
		9+9	stand	-0.18	0.08	34.84	12.00	53.16
			split	-0.10	-	15.13(x2)+13.22(x1)	37.2	19.46(x2)+14.99(x1)
		soft	stand	-0.18	0.08	34.84	12.00	53.16
			hit	-0.10	-	39.28	11.37	49.35
		A+7	DD	-0.29	0.19	38.39	8.70	52.90
	10	hard	stand	-0.24	-	32.35	11.14	56.50
			hit	-0.67	0.43	14.38	3.75	81.86
		9+9	split	-0.44	0.20	11.32(x2)+7.33(x1)	38.5	30.75(x2)+12.09(x1)
		soft	stand	-0.24	0.03	32.35	11.14	56.50
			hit	-0.21	-	34.27	10.49	55.24
		A+7	DD	-0.47	0.26	34.13	8.04	57.83
	A	hard	stand	-0.38	-	24.60	13.08	62.32
			hit	-0.74	0.36	11.71	2.43	85.86
		9+9	split	-0.71	0.33	7.58(x2)+5.30(x1)	35.53	39.50(x2)+12.10(x1)
		soft	stand	-0.38	0.01	24.60	13.08	62.32
			hit	-0.37	-	26.67	9.45	63.88
		A+7	DD	-0.78	0.41	24.60	7.46	63.52

[1] *Mathematical expectation.*
[2] *Average cost of an incorrect decision, in bets lost per hand.*
[3] *Data in percentages, %.*

THE PLAYER HAS 17

With a total of 17 we begin to find ourselves in an unfavourable position for the player, the game situations in which his mathematical expectation is positive are considerably reduced and, even when it is positive, the expected gain is still very close to zero.

Hard and soft hands require different action; always stand if the total is hard but always hit if the total is soft.

In particular, with hard hands where the dealer has a card with a value between 2 and 8, the average loss is relatively low (around 0.1), if however the dealer has an 8, 9, 10 or Ace it increases notably up to 0.64.

With soft hands rather, we can improve our situation by hitting. Therefore we have an expected gain (even if it is very low) if the dealer has a card between 2 and 7; but again, if he has an 8, 9, 10 or Ace we find ourselves in a situation that is not to our advantage.

A+6

In game situations in which it is advantageous to do so, doubling down allows us to improve our expected gain, although still to a very limited extent (+0.15 maximum gain against the dealer's 6). Just as was the case with A+7, doubling down becomes extremely risky in situations that are advantageous to the dealer (8, 9, 10, A).

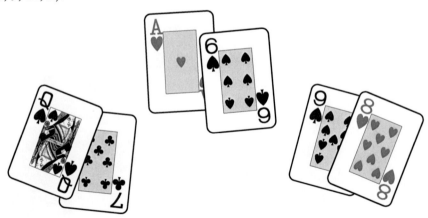

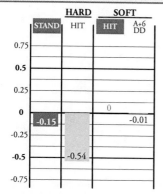

PLAYER 17 - DEALER 2

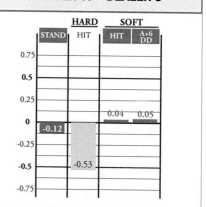

PLAYER 17 - DEALER 3

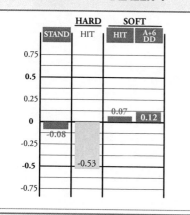

PLAYER 17 - DEALER 4

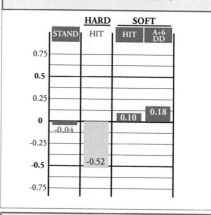

PLAYER 17 - DEALER 5

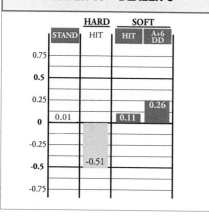

PLAYER 17 - DEALER 6

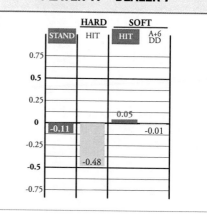

PLAYER 17 - DEALER 7

PLAYER 17 - DEALER 8

PLAYER 17 - DEALER 9

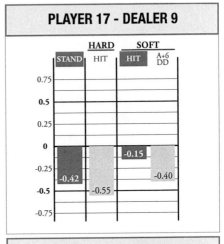

PLAYER 17 - DEALER 10

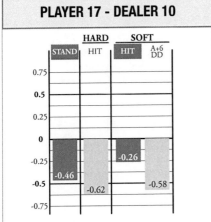

PLAYER 17 - DEALER A

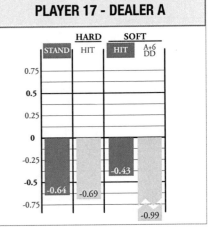

player	dealer	hand	decision	expectation[1]	loss[2]	wins[3]	draws[3]	loses[3]
17	2	hard	stand	-0.15	-	35.36	13.98	50.66
			hit	-0.54	0.39	21.24	3.90	74.86
		soft	stand	-0.15	0.15	35.36	13.98	50.66
			hit	0.00	-	45.69	8.58	45.73
		A+6	DD	-0.01	0.01	45.72	8.20	46.08
	3	hard	stand	-0.12	-	37.37	13.50	49.10
			hit	-0.53	0.41	21.52	3.78	74.70
		soft	stand	-0.12	0.16	37.37	13.50	49.10
			hit	0.04	-	48.19	7.42	44.39
		A+6	hit	0.04	0.01	48.19	7.42	44.39
			DD	0.05	-	47.39	7.93	44.68
	4	hard	stand	-0.08	-	39.45	13.05	47.50
			hit	-0.53	0.45	21.82	3.65	74.52
		soft	stand	-0.08	0.15	39.45	13.05	47.50
			hit	0.07	-	49.99	6.81	43.20
		A+6	hit	0.07	0.05	49.99	6.81	43.20
			DD	0.12	-	49.13	7.67	43.20
	5	hard	stand	-0.04	-	41.64	12.23	46.13
			hit	-0.52	0.48	22.08	3.55	74.37
		soft	stand	-0.04	0.14	41.64	12.23	46.13
			hit	0.10	-	51.74	6.48	41.79
		A+6	hit	0.10	0.08	51.74	6.48	41.79
			DD	0.18	-	50.90	7.31	41.79
	6	hard	stand	0.01	-	42.32	16.54	41.14
			hit	-0.51	0.52	22.98	3.16	73.86
		soft	stand	0.01	0.10	42.32	16.54	41.14
			hit	0.11	-	50.78	9.75	39.47
		A+6	hit	0.11	0.15	50.78	9.75	39.47
			DD	0.26	-	52.28	8.26	39.47
	7	hard	stand	-0.11	-	26.23	36.86	36.91
			hit	-0.48	0.37	24.41	2.84	72.75
		soft	stand	-0.11	0.16	26.23	36.86	36.91
			hit	0.05	-	44.33	16.73	38.95
		A+6	DD	-0.01	0.06	42.57	14.18	43.25
	8	hard	stand	-0.38	-	24.47	12.86	62.67
			hit	-0.51	0.13	22.29	4.82	72.89
		soft	stand	-0.38	0.31	24.47	12.86	62.67
			hit	-0.07	-	40.66	11.38	47.95
		A+6	DD	-0.26	0.19	39.23	8.78	51.99
	9	hard	stand	-0.42	-	22.84	12.00	65.16
			hit	-0.55	0.13	19.81	5.01	75.18
		soft	stand	-0.42	0.27	22.84	12.00	65.16
			hit	-0.15	-	36.85	11.32	51.83
		A+6	DD	-0.40	0.25	35.62	8.70	55.67

player	dealer	hand	decision	expectation[1]	loss[2]	wins[3]	draws[3]	loses[3]
17	10	hard	stand	-0.46	-	21.21	11.14	67.65
			hit	-0.62	0.16	16.87	4.61	78.52
		soft	stand	-0.46	0.20	21.21	11.14	67.65
			hit	-0.26	-	31.85	10.44	57.71
		A+6	DD	-0.58	0.32	31.56	8.04	60.40
	A	hard	stand	-0.64	-	11.52	13.08	75.39
			hit	-0.69	0.05	13.61	3.43	82.96
		soft	stand	-0.64	0.21	11.52	13.08	75.39
			hit	-0.43	-	23.82	9.17	67.01
		A+6	DD	-0.99	0.56	21.58	7.46	70.96

[1] *Mathematical expectation.*

[2] *Average cost of an incorrect decision, in bets lost per hand.*

[3] *Data in percentages, %.*

THE PLAYER HAS 16

Let's get to the heart of the tables.

With 16 the player is bound to lose in the long run, the game situations are in fact almost always disadvantageous, just as in the previous case we have few and limited possibilities for gain with soft hands.

However, by playing correctly we can limit our losses and not hand over money to the casino.

With a hard total we stand if the dealer has a card between 2 and 6 (with an average loss of around 0.20) and we hit if the dealer has 7, 8, 9, 10 or A (a situation that is still very disadvantageous, in fact the average loss is between 0.41 and 0.67), as in this case the dealer has a good chance of closing with at least 17. With a soft total hitting (this will always be the case from now on) is the best option, even if not by a great margin.

A+5

If the dealer has a card of between 2 and 6, the difference between the mathematical expectations of the two possibilities available to us is very slim (0.08 maximum cost of error), however, we see that against a 2 or 3 it is best not to double down, whereas as against a 4, 5 or 6, it becomes the best option. Against a card of 7 or greater on the other hand, doubling down becomes very risky causing us an average loss of between 0.18 against a 7 to 1 against a dealer's Ace.

8+8

In this case splitting is a very advantageous option if the dealer has a card that is 8 or less, in fact for the most part it allows us to improve our situation by moving to a gainful, and therefore favourable, position. Against a 9, the cost of error is limited, only 0.09, but it is nevertheless best to split, moving to an average loss of 0.42 from 0.51. While against a 10 or an Ace it is, as usual, best to do nothing so as not to aggravate an already serious situation.

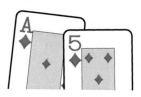

PLAYER 16 - DEALER 2

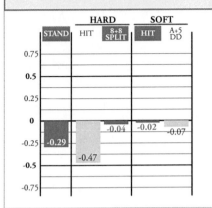

PLAYER 16 - DEALER 3

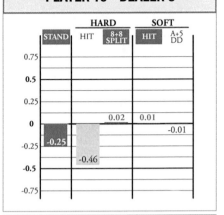

PLAYER 16 - DEALER 4

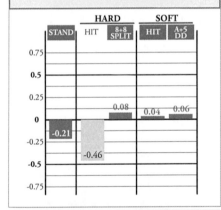

PLAYER 16 - DEALER 5

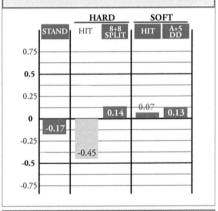

PLAYER 16 - DEALER 6

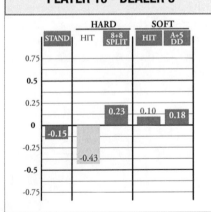

PLAYER 16 - DEALER 7

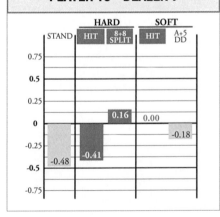

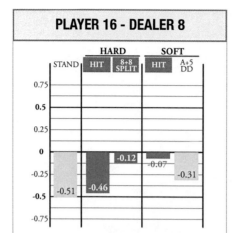

PLAYER 16 - DEALER 8

| | HARD | | SOFT | |
| STAND | HIT | 8+8 SPLIT | HIT | A+5 DD |

- -0.51
- -0.46
- -0.12
- -0.07
- -0.31

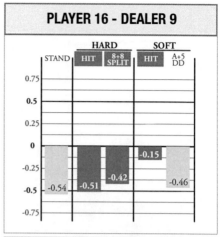

PLAYER 16 - DEALER 9

| | HARD | | SOFT | |
| STAND | HIT | 8+8 SPLIT | HIT | A+5 DD |

- -0.54
- -0.51
- -0.42
- -0.15
- -0.46

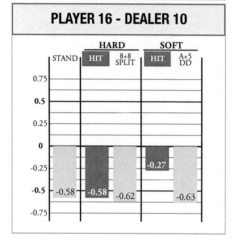

PLAYER 16 - DEALER 10

| | HARD | | SOFT | |
| STAND | HIT | 8+8 SPLIT | HIT | A+5 DD |

- -0.58
- -0.58
- -0.62
- -0.27
- -0.63

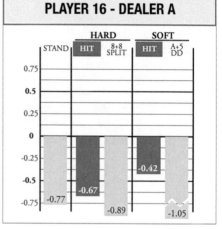

PLAYER 16 - DEALER A

| | HARD | | SOFT | |
| STAND | HIT | 8+8 SPLIT | HIT | A+5 DD |

- -0.77
- -0.67
- -0.89
- -0.42
- -1.05

player	dealer	hand	decision	expectation[1]	loss[2]	wins[3]	draws[3]	loses[3]
16	2	hard	stand	-0.29	-	35.36	0.00	64.64
			hit	-0.47	0.18	23.95	4.97	71.08
		8+8	stand	-0.29	0.21	35.36	0.00	64.64
			split	-0.04	-	20.24(x2)+7.07(x1)	43.05	22.24(x2)+7.41(x1)
		soft	stand	-0.29	0.27	35.36	0.00	64.64
			hit	-0.02	-	46.48	4.94	48.58
		A+5	DD	-0.07	0.05	45.72	4.97	49.30
	3	hard	stand	-0.25	-	37.38	0.00	62.62
			hit	-0.46	0.21	24.40	4.82	70.78
		8+8	stand	-0.25	0.27	37.38	0.00	62.62
			split	0.02	-	21.71(x2)+7.09(x1)	43.26	20.97(x2)+6.96(x1)
		soft	stand	-0.25	0.26	37.38	0.00	62.62
			hit	0.01	-	48.14	4.72	47.15
		A+5	DD	-0.01	0.02	47.39	4.82	47.79
	4	hard	stand	-0.21	-	39.45	0.00	60.55
			hit	-0.46	0.25	24.86	4.66	70.49
		8+8	stand	-0.21	0.29	39.45	0.00	60.55
			split	0.08	-	23.50(x2)+6.72(x1)	43.71	18.89(x2)+6.18(x1)
		soft	stand	-0.21	0.25	39.45	0.00	60.55
			hit	0.04	-	49.94	4.18	45.88
		A+5	hit	0.04	0.02	49.94	4.18	45.88
			DD	0.06	-	49.13	4.66	46.21
	5	hard	stand	-0.17	-	41.64	0.00	58.36
			hit	-0.45	0.28	25.28	4.49	70.23
		8+8	stand	-0.17	0.31	41.64	0.00	58.36
			split	0.14	-	25.20(x2)+6.72(x1)	43.73	18.59(x2)+5.77(x1)
		soft	stand	-0.17	0.24	41.64	0.00	58.36
			hit	0.07	-	51.68	4.05	44.27
		A+5	hit	0.07	0.06	51.68	4.05	44.27
			DD	0.13	-	50.90	4.49	44.61
	6	hard	stand	-0.15	-	42.32	0.00	57.68
			hit	-0.43	0.28	26.24	4.44	69.33
		8+8	stand	-0.15	0.38	42.32	0.00	57.68
			split	0.23	-	27.62(x2)+6.72(x1)	43.56	16.85(x2)+5.25(x1)
		soft	stand	-0.15	0.25	42.32	0.00	57.68
			hit	0.10	-	52.93	3.91	43.16
		A+5	hit	0.10	0.08	52.93	3.91	43.16
			DD	0.18	-	52.28	4.44	43.29
	7	hard	stand	-0.48	0.07	26.23	0.00	73.77
			hit	-0.41	-	26.42	5.67	67.90
		8+8	hit	-0.41	0.57	26.42	5.67	67.90
			split	0.16	-	23.26(x2)+11.34(x1)	39.98	16.01(x2)+9.41(x1)
		soft	stand	-0.48	0.48	26.23	0.00	73.77
			hit	0.00	-	45.77	7.98	46.25
		A+5	DD	-0.18	0.18	42.57	5.67	51.76

player	dealer	hand	decision	expectation[1]	loss[2]	wins[3]	draws[3]	loses[3]
16	8	hard	stand	-0.51	0.05	24.47	0.00	75.53
			hit	-0.46	-	24.17	5.81	70.02
		8+8	hit	-0.46	0.34	24.17	5.81	70.02
			split	-0.12	-	14.76(x2)+13.20(x1)	37.07	19.72(x2)+15.26(x1)
		soft	stand	-0.51	0.44	24.47	0.00	75.53
			hit	-0.07	-	41.84	9.46	48.52
		A+5	DD	-0.31	0.24	39.23	5.81	54.96
	9	hard	stand	-0.54	0.03	22.84	0.00	77.16
			hit	-0.51	-	21.57	5.94	72.50
		8+8	hit	-0.51	0.09	21.57	5.94	72.50
			split	-0.42	-	11.34(x2)+7.83(x1)	38.2	29.92(x2)+12.71(x1)
		soft	stand	-0.54	0.39	22.84	0.00	77.16
			hit	-0.15	-	37.63	9.87	52.50
		A+5	DD	-0.46	0.31	35.62	5.94	58.44
	10	hard	stand	-0.58	0.00	21.21	0.00	78.79
			hit	-0.58	-	18.50	5.47	76.03
		8+8	split	-0.62	0.04	8.91(x2)+5.69(x1)	37.1	36.74(x2)+11.55(x1)
		soft	stand	-0.58	0.31	21.21	0.00	78.79
			hit	-0.27	-	32.04	9.08	58.88
		A+5	DD	-0.63	0.36	31.56	5.47	62.97
	A	hard	stand	-0.77	0.10	11.52	0.00	88.46
			hit	-0.67	-	14.49	4.44	81.07
		8+8	split	-0.89	0.22	5.35(x2)+4.32(x1)	32.1	45.61(x2)+12.62(x1)
		soft	stand	-0.77	0.35	11.52	0.00	88.46
			hit	-0.42	-	25.45	6.87	67.68
		A+5	DD	-1.05	0.63	21.58	4.44	73.98

[1] *Mathematical expectation.*
[2] *Average cost of an incorrect decision, in bets lost per hand.*
[3] *Data in percentages, %.*

THE PLAYER HAS 15

A hard total of 15 presents a very disadvantageous game situation for the player, who will have to follow the strategy in order to minimise his losses; if the total is soft on the other hand there is an opportunity for some small gain (0.12 maximum against the dealer's 6).
The most disadvantageous hands are those where the dealer has a 10 or an Ace.

A+4
With A+4 the strategy is similar to that identified for A+5, only double down against a dealer's 4, 5 or 6, but the gain is still relatively modest (0.06 maximum).

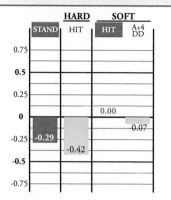

PLAYER 15 - DEALER 2

HARD | SOFT

STAND | HIT | HIT | A+4 DD

0.00
-0.07
-0.29
-0.42

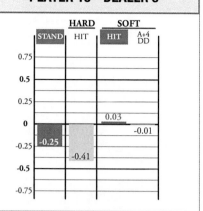

PLAYER 15 - DEALER 3

HARD | SOFT

STAND | HIT | HIT | A+4 DD

0.03
-0.01
-0.25
-0.41

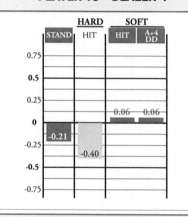

PLAYER 15 - DEALER 4

HARD | SOFT

STAND | HIT | HIT | A+4 DD

0.06 | 0.06
-0.21
-0.40

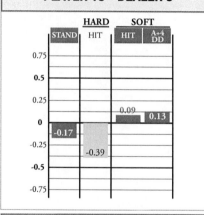

PLAYER 15 - DEALER 5

HARD | SOFT

STAND | HIT | HIT | A+4 DD

0.09 | 0.13
-0.17
-0.39

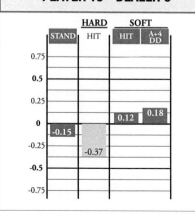

PLAYER 15 - DEALER 6

HARD | SOFT

STAND | HIT | HIT | A+4 DD

0.12 | 0.18
-0.15
-0.37

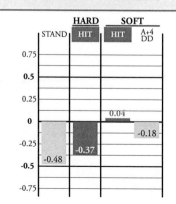

PLAYER 15 - DEALER 7

HARD | SOFT

STAND | HIT | HIT | A+4 DD

0.04
-0.18
-0.48
-0.37

PLAYER 15 - DEALER 8

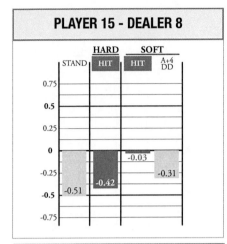

PLAYER 15 - DEALER 9

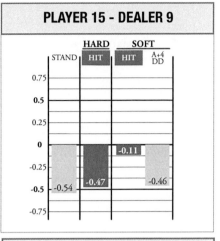

PLAYER 15 - DEALER 10

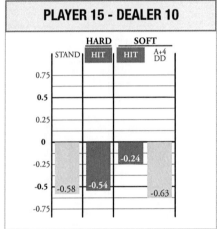

PLAYER 15 - DEALER A

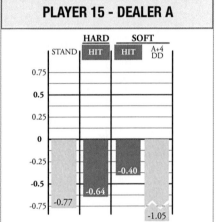

player	dealer	hand	decision	expectation[1]	loss[2]	wins[3]	draws[3]	loses[3]
15	2	hard	stand	-0.29	-	35.36	0.00	64.64
			hit	-0.42	0.13	26.68	4.97	68.34
		soft	stand	-0.29	0.29	35.36	0.00	64.64
			hit	0.00	-	47.34	5.32	47.35
		A+4	DD	-0.07	0.07	45.72	4.97	49.30
	3	hard	stand	-0.25	-	37.38	0.00	62.62
			hit	-0.41	0.16	27.28	4.82	67.91
		soft	stand	-0.25	0.28	37.38	0.00	62.62
			hit	0.03	-	48.96	5.08	45.96
		A+4	DD	-0.01	0.04	47.39	4.82	47.79
	4	hard	stand	-0.21	-	39.45	0.00	60.55
			hit	-0.40	0.19	27.89	4.66	67.45
		soft	stand	-0.21	0.27	39.45	0.00	60.55
			hit	0.06	-	50.75	4.50	44.75
		A+4	hit	0.06	0.00	50.75	4.50	44.75
			DD	0.06	-	49.13	4.66	46.21
	5	hard	stand	-0.17	-	41.64	0.00	58.36
			hit	-0.39	0.22	28.48	4.49	67.03
		soft	stand	-0.17	0.26	42.32	0.00	57.68
			hit	0.09	-	52.45	4.36	43.19
		A+4	hit	0.09	-	52.45	4.36	43.19
			DD	0.13	-	50.90	4.49	44.61
	6	hard	stand	-0.15	-	42.32	0.00	57.68
			hit	-0.37	0.22	29.49	4.44	66.07
		soft	stand	-0.15	0.27	42.32	0.00	57.68
			hit	0.12	-	53.74	4.22	42.04
		A+4	hit	0.12	-	53.74	4.22	42.04
			DD	0.18	-	52.28	4.44	43.29
	7	hard	stand	-0.48	0.11	26.23	0.00	73.77
			hit	-0.37	-	28.46	6.11	65.43
		soft	stand	-0.48	0.52	26.23	0.00	73.77
			hit	0.04	-	47.72	8.26	44.02
		A+4	DD	-0.18	0.22	42.57	5.67	51.76
	8	hard	stand	-0.51	0.09	24.47	0.00	75.53
			hit	-0.42	-	26.03	6.26	67.71
		soft	stand	-0.51	0.48	24.47	0.00	75.53
			hit	-0.03	-	43.63	10.04	46.33
		A+4	DD	-0.31	0.28	39.23	5.81	54.96
	9	hard	stand	-0.54	0.07	22.84	0.00	77.16
			hit	-0.47	-	23.23	6.39	70.38
		soft	stand	-0.54	0.43	22.84	0.00	77.16
			hit	-0.11	-	39.25	10.27	50.47
		A+4	DD	-0.46	0.35	35.62	5.94	58.44

player	dealer	hand	decision	expectation[1]	loss[2]	wins[3]	draws[3]	loses[3]
	10	hard	stand	-0.58	0.04	21.21	0.00	78.79
			hit	-0.54	-	19.93	5.89	74.18
		soft	stand	-0.58	0.34	21.21	0.00	78.79
			hit	-0.24	-	33.41	9.46	57.14
		A+4	DD	-0.63	0.39	31.56	5.47	62.97
	A	hard	stand	-0.77	0.13	11.52	0.00	88.46
			hit	-0.64	-	15.61	4.78	79.61
		soft	stand	-0.77	0.37	11.52	0.00	88.46
			hit	-0.40	-	26.55	7.14	66.32
		A+4	DD	-1.05	0.65	21.58	4.44	73.98

[1] *Mathematical expectation.*

[2] *Average cost of an incorrect decision, in bets lost per hand.*

[3] *Data in percentages, %.*

THE PLAYER HAS 14

> **HIT WITH HARD HAND AGAINST 7, 8, 9, 10, A**
> **SPLIT WITH 7+7 AGAINST 2, 3, 4, 5, 6, 7**
> **HIT WITH SOFT HAND**
> **DOUBLE DOWN WITH A+3 AGAINST 5, 6**

Compared to totals of 15 and 16, the percentages for hitting are gradually improving since the chances of going bust decrease as the players total decreases.

A+3
Against a card with a value of 6 or less, doubling down or not, as the case may be, does not greatly alter the expected gain (variations of around 0.1), but the maths suggests only doubling down against the dealer's 5 or 6.
If the dealer has a card of 7 or greater instead, doubling down becomes a completely absurd choice.

7+7
Split against a 2, 3, 4, 5, 6 or 7; in these cases dividing the pair of 7's improves our expected gain by approximately 10-20 hundredths of the bet, against a 6 we even move into a position that is slightly advantageous for the player.
However, against an 8 or greater, don't split but hit!

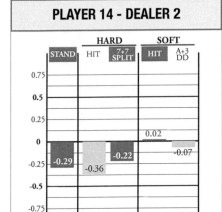

PLAYER 14 - DEALER 2

	HARD		SOFT	
STAND	HIT	7+7 SPLIT	HIT	A+3 DD

- 0.02
- -0.29
- -0.36
- -0.22
- -0.07

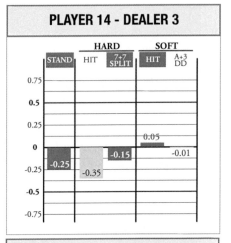

PLAYER 14 - DEALER 3

	HARD		SOFT	
STAND	HIT	7+7 SPLIT	HIT	A+3 DD

- 0.05
- -0.25
- -0.35
- -0.15
- -0.01

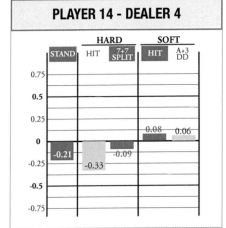

PLAYER 14 - DEALER 4

	HARD		SOFT	
STAND	HIT	7+7 SPLIT	HIT	A+3 DD

- 0.08
- 0.06
- -0.21
- -0.33
- -0.09

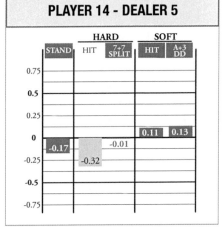

PLAYER 14 - DEALER 5

	HARD		SOFT	
STAND	HIT	7+7 SPLIT	HIT	A+3 DD

- 0.11
- 0.13
- -0.17
- -0.32
- -0.01

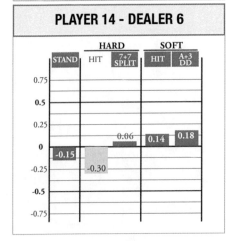

PLAYER 14 - DEALER 6

	HARD		SOFT	
STAND	HIT	7+7 SPLIT	HIT	A+3 DD

- 0.06
- 0.14
- 0.18
- -0.15
- -0.30

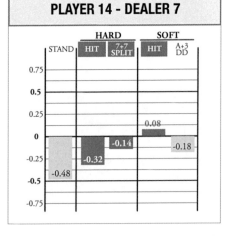

PLAYER 14 - DEALER 7

	HARD		SOFT	
STAND	HIT	7+7 SPLIT	HIT	A+3 DD

- 0.08
- -0.14
- -0.18
- -0.48
- -0.32

PLAYER 14 - DEALER 8

HARD | SOFT
STAND | HIT | 7+7 SPLIT | HIT | A+3 DD

- STAND: -0.51
- HIT (HARD): -0.37
- 7+7 SPLIT: -0.42
- HIT (SOFT): 0.01
- A+3 DD: -0.31

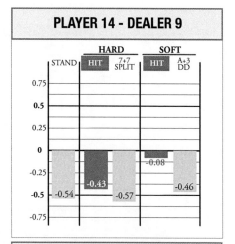

PLAYER 14 - DEALER 9

HARD | SOFT
STAND | HIT | 7+7 SPLIT | HIT | A+3 DD

- STAND: -0.54
- HIT (HARD): -0.43
- 7+7 SPLIT: -0.57
- HIT (SOFT): -0.08
- A+3 DD: -0.46

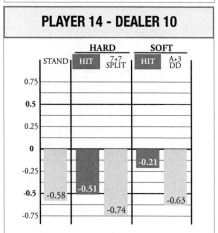

PLAYER 14 - DEALER 10

HARD | SOFT
STAND | HIT | 7+7 SPLIT | HIT | A+3 DD

- STAND: -0.58
- HIT (HARD): -0.51
- 7+7 SPLIT: -0.74
- HIT (SOFT): -0.21
- A+3 DD: -0.63

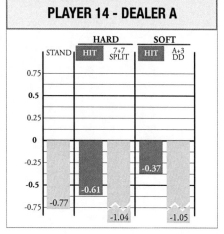

PLAYER 14 - DEALER A

HARD | SOFT
STAND | HIT | 7+7 SPLIT | HIT | A+3 DD

- STAND: -0.77
- HIT (HARD): -0.61
- 7+7 SPLIT: -1.04
- HIT (SOFT): -0.37
- A+3 DD: -1.05

player	dealer	hand	decision	expectation[1]	loss[2]	wins[3]	draws[3]	loses[3]
14	2	hard	stand	-0.29	-	35.36	0.00	64.64
			hit	-0.36	0.07	29.40	4.97	65.62
		7+7	stand	-0.29	0.07	35.36	0.00	64.64
			split	-0.22	-	16.60(x2)+6.19(x1)	42.68	26.69(x2)+7.85(x1)
		soft	stand	-0.29	0.31	35.36	0.00	64.64
			hit	0.02	-	48.26	5.73	46.02
		A+3	DD	-0.07	0.09	45.72	4.97	49.30
	3	hard	stand	-0.25	-	37.38	0.00	62.62
			hit	-0.35	0.10	30.16	4.82	65.03
		7+7	stand	-0.25	0.10	37.38	0.00	62.62
			split	-0.15	-	18.06(x2)+6.24(x1)	43.16	25.15(x2)+7.37(x1)
		soft	stand	-0.25	0.30	37.38	0.00	62.62
			hit	0.05	-	49.85	5.47	44.68
		A+3	DD	-0.01	0.06	47.39	4.82	47.79
	4	hard	stand	-0.21	-	39.45	0.00	60.55
			hit	-0.33	0.12	30.93	4.66	64.42
		7+7	stand	-0.21	0.12	39.45	0.00	60.55
			split	-0.09	-	19.82(x2)+5.93(x1)	43.92	23.84(x2)+6.50(x1)
		soft	stand	-0.21	0.29	39.45	0.00	60.55
			hit	0.08	-	51.62	4.85	43.53
		A+3	DD	0.06	0.02	49.13	4.66	46.21
	5	hard	stand	-0.17	-	41.64	0.00	58.36
			hit	-0.32	0.15	31.69	4.49	63.83
		7+7	stand	-0.17	0.16	41.64	0.00	58.36
			split	-0.01	-	21.60(x2)+5.87(x1)	44.28	22.28(x2)+5.96(x1)
		soft	stand	-0.17	0.28	41.64	0.00	58.36
			hit	0.11	-	53.29	4.69	42.02
		A+3	hit	0.11	0.02	53.29	4.69	42.02
			DD	0.13	-	50.90	4.49	44.61
	6	hard	stand	-0.15	-	42.32	0.00	57.68
			hit	-0.30	0.15	32.75	4.44	62.82
		7+7	hit	-0.30	0.21	32.75	4.44	62.82
			split	0.06	-	22.78(x2)+7.12(x1)	43.34	20.08(x2)+6.68(x1)
		soft	stand	-0.15	0.29	42.32	0.00	57.68
			hit	0.14	-	54.62	4.54	40.84
		A+3	hit	0.14	0.04	54.62	4.54	40.84
			DD	0.18	-	52.28	4.44	43.29
	7	hard	stand	-0.48	0.16	26.23	0.00	73.77
			hit	-0.32	-	30.65	6.58	62.77
		7+7	hit	-0.32	0.18	30.65	6.58	62.77
			split	-0.14	-	14.38(x2)+13.10(x1)	36.97	20.08(x2)+15.47(x1)
		soft	stand	-0.48	0.56	26.23	0.00	73.77
			hit	0.08	-	49.71	8.53	41.76
		A+3	DD	-0.18	0.26	42.57	5.67	51.76

player	dealer	hand	decision	expectation[1]	loss[2]	wins[3]	draws[3]	loses[3]
14	8	hard	stand	-0.51	0.14	24.47	0.00	75.53
			hit	-0.37	-	28.04	6.74	65.23
		7+7	split	-0.42	0.05	11.28(x2)+7.90(x1)	38.1	29.87(x2)+12.85(x1)
		soft	stand	-0.51	0.52	24.47	0.00	75.53
			hit	0.01	-	45.44	10.44	44.11
		A+3	DD	-0.31	0.32	39.23	5.81	54.96
	9	hard	stand	-0.54	0.11	22.84	0.00	77.16
			hit	-0.43	-	25.01	6.88	68.10
		7+7	split	-0.57	0.14	9.39(x2)+6.24(x1)	37.3	35.02(x2)+12.05(x1)
		soft	stand	-0.54	0.46	22.84	0.00	77.16
			hit	-0.08	-	40.90	10.69	48.42
		A+3	DD	-0.46	0.38	35.62	5.94	58.44
	10	hard	stand	-0.58	0.07	21.21	0.00	78.79
			hit	-0.51	-	21.46	6.34	72.20
		7+7	split	-0.74	0.23	7.12(x2)+5.05(x1)	34.97	40.79(x2)+12.08(x1)
		soft	stand	-0.58	0.37	21.21	0.00	78.79
			hit	-0.21	-	34.80	9.83	55.37
		A+3	DD	-0.63	0.42	31.56	5.47	62.97
	A	hard	stand	-0.77	0.16	11.52	0.00	88.46
			hit	-0.61	-	16.81	5.15	78.04
		7+7	split	-1.04	0.43	3.80(x2)+3.43(x1)	28.72	51.43(x2)+12.62(x1)
		soft	stand	-0.77	0.40	11.52	0.00	88.46
			hit	-0.37	-	27.66	7.40	64.93
		A+3	DD	-1.05	0.68	21.58	4.44	73.98

[1] *Mathematical expectation.*

[2] *Average cost of an incorrect decision, in bets lost per hand.*

[3] *Data in percentages, %.*

THE PLAYER HAS 13

Again, with hard totals we must stand against 2, 3, 4, 5 and 6 but the cost of error has now decreased notably, it now varies from 0.02 against the dealer's 2, to 0.09 against a 6.

From 7 or greater we must hit instead and in these situations an error becomes more significant, going bust at this point would mean handing over an average of 20 hundredths of the bet to the casino per hand.

With soft totals we will hit as usual, with limited prospects for gain, against the dealer's 8 or less.

A+2

Just as with A+3, the calculation tells us only to double down against a dealer's 5 or 6. There are however cases in which the difference between the two options is minimal and choosing to double down does not greatly improve the expected gain.

PLAYER 13 - DEALER 2

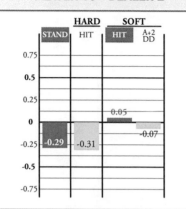

PLAYER 13 - DEALER 3

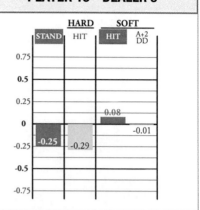

PLAYER 13 - DEALER 4

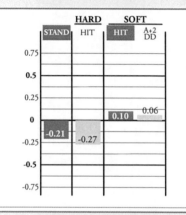

PLAYER 13 - DEALER 5

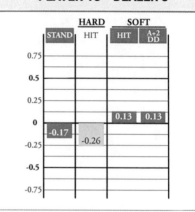

PLAYER 13 - DEALER 6

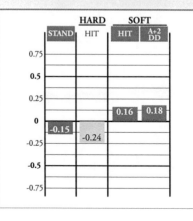

PLAYER 13 - DEALER 7

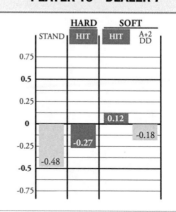

PLAYER 13 - DEALER 8

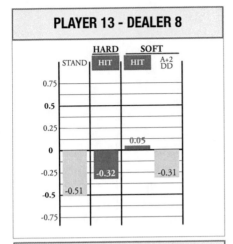

PLAYER 13 - DEALER 9

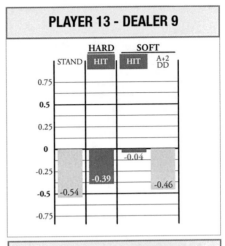

PLAYER 13 - DEALER 10

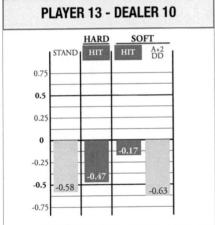

PLAYER 13 - DEALER A

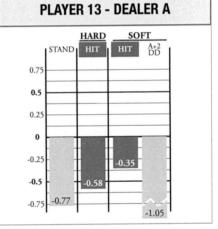

player	dealer	hand	decision	expectation[1]	loss[2]	wins[3]	draws[3]	loses[3]
13	2	hard	stand	-0.29	-	35.36	0.00	64.64
			hit	-0.31	0.02	32.12	4.97	62.90
		soft	stand	-0.29	0.34	35.36	0.00	64.64
			hit	0.05	-	49.25	6.17	44.58
		A+2	DD	-0.07	0.12	45.72	4.97	49.30
	3	hard	stand	-0.25	-	37.38	0.00	62.62
			hit	-0.29	0.04	33.03	4.82	62.15
		soft	stand	-0.29	0.37	37.38	0.00	62.62
			hit	0.08	-	50.81	5.89	43.30
		A+2	DD	-0.01	0.09	47.39	4.82	47.79
	4	hard	stand	-0.21	-	39.45	0.00	60.55
			hit	-0.27	0.06	33.96	4.66	61.38
		soft	stand	-0.21	0.31	39.45	0.00	60.55
			hit	0.10	-	52.56	5.22	42.23
		A+2	DD	0.06	0.04	49.13	4.66	46.21
	5	hard	stand	-0.17	-	41.64	0.00	58.36
			hit	-0.26	0.09	34.89	4.49	60.62
		soft	stand	-0.17	0.30	41.64	0.00	58.36
			hit	0.13	-	54.18	5.05	40.76
		A+2	hit	0.13	0.00	54.18	5.05	40.76
			DD	0.13	-	50.90	4.49	44.61
	6	hard	stand	-0.15	-	42.32	0.00	57.68
			hit	-0.24	0.09	36.00	4.44	59.56
		soft	stand	-0.15	0.31	42.32	0.00	57.68
			hit	0.16	-	55.57	4.89	39.54
		A+2	hit	0.16	0.02	55.57	4.89	39.54
			DD	0.18	-	52.28	4.44	43.29
	7	hard	stand	-0.48	0.21	26.23	0.00	73.77
			hit	-0.27	-	33.00	7.09	59.91
		soft	stand	-0.48	0.60	26.23	0.00	73.77
			hit	0.12	-	51.72	8.80	39.48
		A+2	DD	-0.18	0.30	42.57	5.67	51.76
	8	hard	stand	-0.51	0.19	24.47	0.00	75.53
			hit	-0.32	-	30.19	7.26	62.55
		soft	stand	-0.51	0.56	24.47	0.00	75.53
			hit	0.05	-	47.28	10.84	41.87
		A+2	DD	-0.31	0.36	39.23	5.81	54.96
	9	hard	stand	-0.54	0.15	22.84	0.00	77.16
			hit	-0.39	-	26.94	7.41	65.65
		soft	stand	-0.54	0.50	22.84	0.00	77.16
			hit	-0.04	-	42.57	11.10	46.33
		A+2	DD	-0.46	0.42	35.62	5.94	58.44

player	dealer	hand	decision	expectation[1]	loss[2]	wins[3]	draws[3]	loses[3]
13	10	hard	stand	-0.58	0.11	21.21	0.00	78.79
			hit	-0.47	-	23.11	6.83	70.06
		soft	stand	-0.58	0.41	21.21	0.00	78.79
			hit	-0.17	-	36.21	10.22	53.58
		A+2	DD	-0.63	0.46	31.56	5.47	62.97
	A	hard	stand	-0.77	0.19	11.52	0.00	88.46
			hit	-0.58	-	18.10	5.54	76.35
		soft	stand	-0.77	0.42	11.52	0.00	88.46
			hit	-0.35	-	28.80	7.67	63.53
		A+2	DD	-1.05	0.70	21.58	4.44	73.98

[1] *Mathematical expectation.*
[2] *Average cost of an incorrect decision, in bets lost per hand.*
[3] *Data in percentages, %.*

THE PLAYER HAS 12

While with a hard total between 16 and 13 the player must always stand against the dealer's 2 or 3, with 12 things change. We have seen that as the player's total decreases so too do the chances of him going bust and consequently the mathematical expectation of hitting increases; we see that with a total of 12 against 2 or 3 this becomes greater than the mathematical expectation of standing, though not by much.

6+6
If the initial cards are two 6's, the player should split against 3, 4, 5 or 6. However an incorrect decision does not cost much when the dealer has less than 8 (0.1 on average), while against a 9, 10 or Ace splitting would mean the player giving the casino much more money.

A+A
A soft 12 can only be obtained by the sum of two Aces, in this case the player can split or hit. We do not even consider the option of standing because the player can only improve his total by hitting, therefore it would make no sense not to do so and be content with a lower total.
Looking at the data in the tables that follow we see that splitting greatly increases our expected gain: by approximately 50 hundredths of the bet, if the dealer has a card that is less than 8 and approximately 20 hundredths of the bet against an 8, 9 or 10, meaning we are always in game situations that are favourable to the player. Only against the dealer's Ace should we not split the pair of Aces as in this case we would move from an average loss of 0.32 hundredths of the bet to a loss of 0.35 hundredths of the bet.

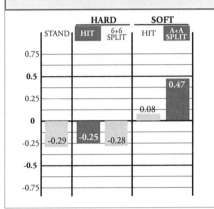

PLAYER 12 - DEALER 2

HARD · SOFT

STAND · HIT · 6+6 SPLIT · HIT · A+A SPLIT

- 0.47
- 0.08
- -0.29
- -0.25
- -0.28

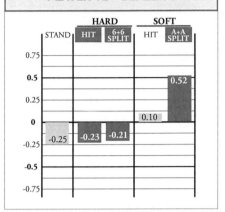

PLAYER 12 - DEALER 3

HARD · SOFT

STAND · HIT · 6+6 SPLIT · HIT · A+A SPLIT

- 0.52
- 0.10
- -0.25
- -0.23
- -0.21

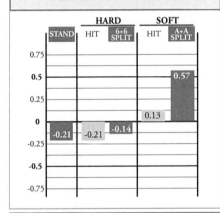

PLAYER 12 - DEALER 4

HARD · SOFT

STAND · HIT · 6+6 SPLIT · HIT · A+A SPLIT

- 0.57
- 0.13
- -0.21
- -0.21
- -0.14

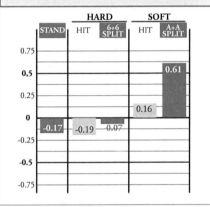

PLAYER 12 - DEALER 5

HARD · SOFT

STAND · HIT · 6+6 SPLIT · HIT · A+A SPLIT

- 0.61
- 0.16
- -0.17
- -0.19
- -0.07

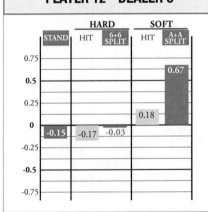

PLAYER 12 - DEALER 6

HARD · SOFT

STAND · HIT · 6+6 SPLIT · HIT · A+A SPLIT

- 0.67
- 0.18
- -0.15
- -0.17
- -0.03

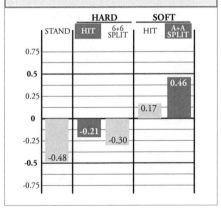

PLAYER 12 - DEALER 7

HARD · SOFT

STAND · HIT · 6+6 SPLIT · HIT · A+A SPLIT

- 0.46
- 0.17
- -0.21
- -0.30
- -0.48

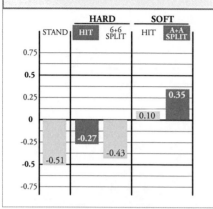

PLAYER 12 - DEALER 8

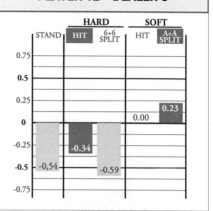

PLAYER 12 - DEALER 9

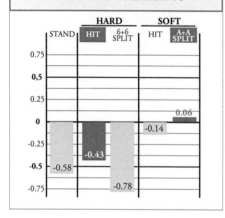

PLAYER 12 - DEALER 10

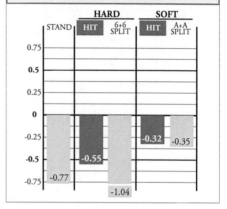

PLAYER 12 - DEALER A

player	dealer	hand	decision	expectation[1]	loss[2]	wins[3]	draws[3]	loses[3]
12	2	hard	stand	-0.29	0.04	35.36	0.00	64.64
			hit	-0.25	-	34.84	4.97	60.18
		6+6	split	-0.28	0.03	16.98(x2)+2.90(x1)	45.68	30.56(x2)+3.89(x1)
		A+A	hit	0.08	0.39	50.20	7.79	42.01
			split	0.47	-	33.54(x2)+8.91(x1)	40.42	11.82(x2)+5.29(x1)
	3	hard	stand	-0.25	0.02	37.38	0.00	62.62
			hit	-0.23	-	35.91	4.82	59.28
		6+6	hit	-0.23	0.02	35.91	4.82	59.28
			split	-0.21	-	18.49(x2)+2.87(x1)	46.25	28.79(x2)+3.59(x1)
		A+A	hit	0.10	0.42	51.50	7.46	41.05
			split	0.52	-	35.05(x2)+8.83(x1)	40.03	11.11(x2)+4.97(x1)
	4	hard	stand	-0.21	-	39.45	0.00	60.55
			hit	-0.21	0.00	36.99	4.66	58.35
		6+6	stand	-0.21	0.07	39.45	0.00	60.55
			split	-0.14	-	20.27(x2)+2.46(x1)	47.12	27.30(x2)+2.85(x1)
		A+A	hit	0.13	0.44	53.56	5.62	40.82
			split	0.57	-	36.65(x2)+8.75(x1)	39.55	10.39(x2)+4.66(x1)
	5	hard	stand	-0.17	-	41.64	0.00	58.36
			hit	-0.19	0.02	38.09	4.49	57.42
		6+6	stand	-0.17	0.10	41.64	0.00	58.36
			split	-0.07	-	22.06(x2)+2.47(x1)	47.42	25.40(x2)+2.65(x1)
		A+A	hit	0.16	0.45	55.15	5.44	39.41
			split	0.61	-	38.28(x2)+8.65(x1)	39.02	9.70(x2)+4.35(x1)
	6	hard	stand	-0.15	-	42.32	0.00	57.68
			hit	-0.17	0.02	39.26	4.44	56.31
		6+6	stand	-0.15	0.12	42.32	0.00	57.68
			split	-0.03	-	22.94(x2)+2.67(x1)	47.32	24.32(x2)+2.75(x1)
		A+A	hit	0.18	0.49	56.59	5.27	38.15
			split	0.67	-	40.13(x2)+8.46(x1)	38.42	8.99(x2)+4.00(x1)
	7	hard	stand	-0.48	0.27	26.23	0.00	73.77
			hit	-0.21	-	35.54	7.63	56.83
		6+6	split	-0.30	0.09	14.61(x2)+6.40(x1)	41.53	28.53(x2)+8.94(x1)
		A+A	hit	0.17	0.29	53.75	9.06	37.20
			split	0.46	-	33.50(x2)+8.55(x1)	40.76	12.07(x2)+5.13(x1)
	8	hard	stand	-0.51	0.24	24.47	0.00	75.53
			hit	-0.27	-	32.51	7.81	59.67
		6+6	split	-0.43	0.16	12.14(x2)+5.98(x1)	40.17	32.00(x2)+9.71(x1)
		A+A	hit	0.10	0.25	49.13	11.25	39.62
			split	0.35	-	30.32(x2)+8.16(x1)	41.88	14.08(x2)+5.56(x1)
	9	hard	stand	-0.54	0.20	22.84	0.00	77.16
			hit	-0.34	-	29.01	7.98	63.01
		6+6	split	-0.59	0.25	9.61(x2)+5.42(x1)	38.12	36.31(x2)+10.54(x1)
		A+A	hit	0.00	0.23	44.25	11.52	44.24
			split	0.23	-	27.07(x2)+7.64(x1)	42.82	16.51(x2)+5.96(x1)

player	dealer	hand	decision	expectation[1]	loss[2]	wins[3]	draws[3]	loses[3]
		hard	stand	-0.58	0.15	21.21	0.00	78.79
			hit	-0.43	-	24.89	7.36	67.75
	10	6+6	split	-0.78	0.35	7.04(x2)+4.26(x1)	35.37	42.83(x2)+10.50(x1)
		A+A	hit	-0.14	0.20	37.62	10.60	51.78
			split	0.06	-	22.25(x2)+8.14(x1)	42.44	19.54(x2)+7.63(x1)
		hard	stand	-0.77	0.22	11.52	0.00	88.46
			hit	-0.55	-	19.50	5.97	74.53
	A	6+6	split	-1.04	0.49	4.34(x2)+2.71(x1)	30.71	52.80(x2)+9.44(x1)
		A+A	hit	-0.32	-	29.94	7.93	62.13
			split	-0.35	0.03	11.33(x2)+10.20(x1)	36.76	26.21(x2)+15.51(x1)

[1] *Mathematical expectation.*

[2] *Average cost of an incorrect decision, in bets lost per hand.*

[3] *Data in percentages, %.*

THE PLAYER HAS 11

With totals of 11 or less the option of standing no longer makes any sense, as hitting can only increase the total. From now on soft hands no longer exist.
The real choice with a total of 11 is between hitting and doubling down (when possible) and in fact doubling down is often the best choice. The average gain doubles if the dealer has a card between 2 and 7 and increases against an 8 or 9. Against a 10 or Ace, it is best to hit because the situation is favourable to the dealer.

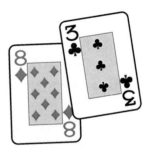

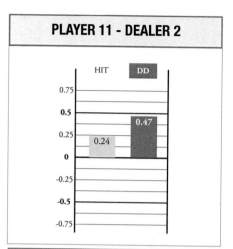

PLAYER 11 - DEALER 2

HIT   DD

0.24   0.47

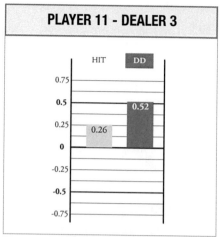

PLAYER 11 - DEALER 3

HIT   DD

0.26   0.52

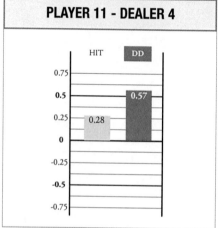

PLAYER 11 - DEALER 4

HIT   DD

0.28   0.57

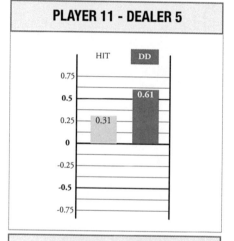

PLAYER 11 - DEALER 5

HIT   DD

0.31   0.61

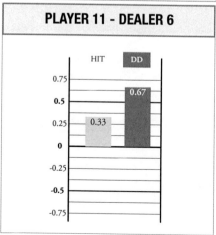

PLAYER 11 - DEALER 6

HIT   DD

0.33   0.67

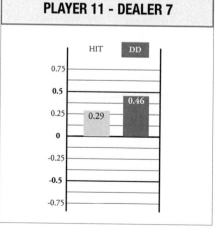

PLAYER 11 - DEALER 7

HIT   DD

0.29   0.46

GIOCATORE 11 - DEALER 8

HIT DD

0.75
0.5
0.25   0.23 0.35
0
-0.25
-0.5
-0.75

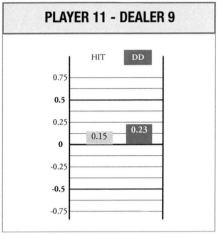

PLAYER 11 - DEALER 9

HIT DD

0.75
0.5
0.25   0.23
0   0.15
-0.25
-0.5
-0.75

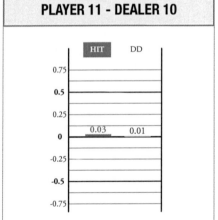

PLAYER 11 - DEALER 10

HIT DD

0.75
0.5
0.25
0   0.03   0.01
-0.25
-0.5
-0.75

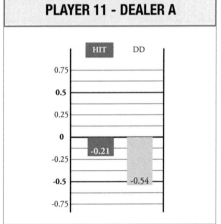

PLAYER 11 - DEALER A

HIT DD

0.75
0.5
0.25
0
-0.25 -0.21
-0.5   -0.54
-0.75

player	dealer	hand	decision	expectation[1]	loss[2]	wins[3]	draws[3]	loses[3]
11	2	hard	hit	0.24	0.23	57.88	8.08	34.04
			DD	0.47	-	57.92	7.70	34.39
	3	hard	hit	0.26	0.26	59.10	7.83	33.07
			DD	0.52	-	59.19	7.46	33.35
	4	hard	hit	0.28	0.29	60.54	7.22	32.24
			DD	0.57	-	60.54	7.22	32.24
	5	hard	hit	0.31	0.30	61.87	6.99	31.14
			DD	0.61	-	61.87	6.99	31.14
	6	hard	hit	0.33	0.34	63.34	6.68	29.98
			DD	0.67	-	63.34	6.68	29.98
	7	hard	hit	0.29	0.17	59.64	9.93	30.43
			DD	0.46	-	57.88	7.38	34.74
	8	hard	hit	0.23	0.12	56.49	10.02	33.49
			DD	0.35	-	55.06	7.41	37.53
	9	hard	hit	0.15	0.12	52.91	10.00	37.09
			DD	0.23	-	52.03	7.34	40.64
	10	hard	hit	0.03	-	47.31	8.72	43.97
			DD	0.01	0.02	47.17	6.27	46.57
	A	hard	hit	-0.21	-	35.73	7.67	56.60
			DD	-0.54	0.33	33.65	5.68	60.67

[1] *Mathematical expectation.*

[2] *Average cost of an incorrect decision, in bets lost per hand.*

[3] *Data in percentages, %.*

THE PLAYER HAS 10

With a total of 10 the same applies, the choice is between hitting and doubling down.

Against the dealer's card of between 2 and 9 doubling down is advantageous, because we are in an area that is favourable to the player; against 10 and Ace it is favourable to the dealer, so it is best to limit yourself to hitting.

5+5

When the player has two 5's in hand he can also decide to split, but as starting with 10 is in general advantageous to the player (who also has the chance to double down), a pair of 5's is never split. In fact, from the data that follows we can see that this choice always leads to a negative mathematical expectation that is much less compared to the other two options.

PLAYER 10 - DEALER 2

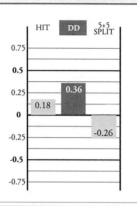

PLAYER 10 - DEALER 3

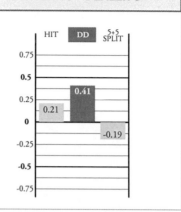

PLAYER 10 - DEALER 4

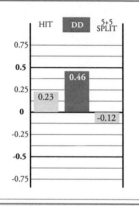

PLAYER 10 - DEALER 5

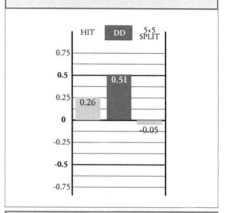

PLAYER 10 - DEALER 6

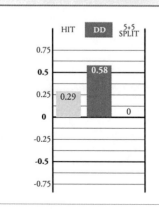

PLAYER 10 - DEALER 7

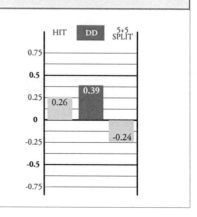

PLAYER 10 - DEALER 8

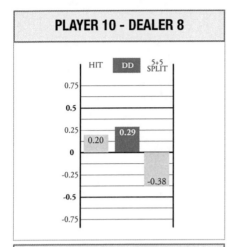

PLAYER 10 - DEALER 9

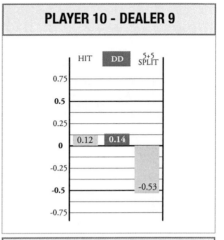

PLAYER 10 - DEALER 10

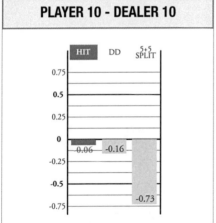

PLAYER 10 - DEALER A

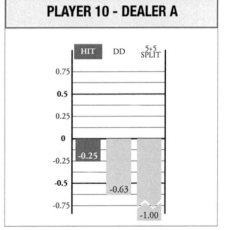

player	dealer	hand	decision	expectation[1]	loss[2]	wins[3]	draws[3]	loses[3]
10	2	hard	hit	0.18	0.18	55.02	8.22	36.77
			DD	0.36	-	55.05	7.83	37.11
		5+5	split	-0.26	0.62	17.37(x2)+3.19(x1)	45.58	29.70(x2)+4.17(x1)
	3	hard	hit	0.21	0.20	56.33	7.96	35.71
			DD	0.41	-	56.42	7.59	35.99
		5+5	split	-0.19	0.60	18.83(x2)+3.21(x1)	46.05	27.99(x2)+3.91(x1)
	4	hard	hit	0.23	0.23	57.85	7.35	34.80
			DD	0.46	-	57.85	7.35	34.80
		5+5	split	-0.12	0.58	20.62(x2)+2.76(x1)	46.91	26.58(x2)+3.13(x1)
	5	hard	hit	0.26	0.25	59.26	7.10	33.64
			DD	0.51	-	59.26	7.10	33.64
		5+5	split	-0.05	0.56	22.41(x2)+2.77(x1)	47.17	24.73(x2)+2.91(x1)
	6	hard	hit	0.29	0.29	61.00	6.78	32.22
			DD	0.58	-	61.00	6.78	32.22
		5+5	split	0.00	0.58	23.50(x2)+2.83(x1)	47.21	23.63(x2)+2.83(x1)
	7	hard	hit	0.26	0.13	57.83	10.03	32.14
			DD	0.39	-	56.07	7.49	36.45
		5+5	split	-0.24	0.63	15.75(x2)+6.90(x1)	41.73	26.66(x2)+8.97(x1)
	8	hard	hit	0.20	0.09	54.89	10.02	35.09
			DD	0.29	-	53.46	7.41	39.13
		5+5	split	-0.38	0.67	13.03(x2)+6.50(x1)	40.44	30.14(x2)+9.89(x1)
	9	hard	hit	0.12	0.02	50.14	11.37	38.49
			DD	0.14	-	49.26	8.70	42.04
		5+5	split	-0.53	0.67	10.33(x2)+5.83(x1)	38.61	34.57(x2)+10.66(x1)
	10	hard	hit	-0.06	-	38.82	16.41	44.77
			DD	-0.16	0.10	39.27	13.37	47.36
		5+5	split	-0.73	0.67	7.56(x2)+4.58(x1)	35.99	41.19(x2)+10.68(x1)
	A	hard	hit	-0.25	-	32.71	9.45	57.84
			DD	-0.63	0.38	30.64	7.46	61.91
		5+5	split	-1.00	0.75	4.67(x2)+2.91(x1)	31.42	51.35(x2)+9.65(x1)

[1] Mathematical expectation.
[2] Average cost of an incorrect decision, in bets lost per hand.
[3] Data in percentages, %.

THE PLAYER HAS 9

With a total of 9 the same goes as for 10 and 11, the choice is between hitting and doubling down.

The choice between the two options is however more varied than the preceding cases, the occasions on which it is best to limit oneself to hitting increase, while doubling down is only advantageous against 3, 4, 5 and 6.

PLAYER 9 - DEALER 2

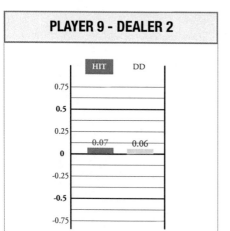

PLAYER 9 - DEALER 3

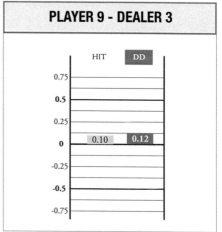

PLAYER 9 - DEALER 4

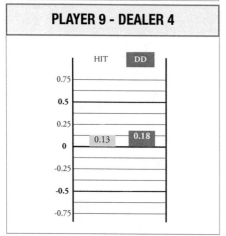

PLAYER 9 - DEALER 5

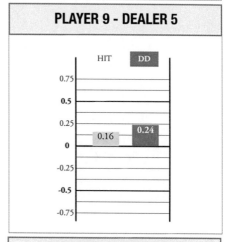

PLAYER 9 - DEALER 6

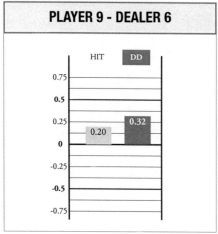

PLAYER 9 - DEALER 7

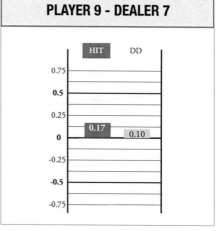

PLAYER 9 - DEALER 8

PLAYER 9 - DEALER 9

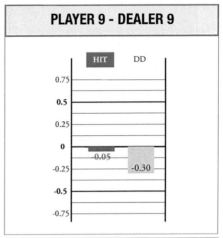

PLAYER 9 - DEALER 10

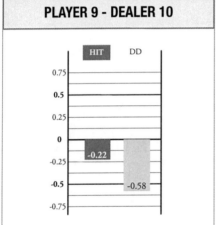

PLAYER 9 - DEALER A

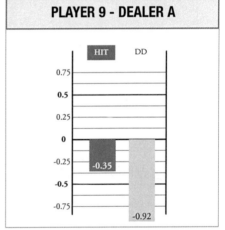

player	dealer	hand	decision	expectation[1]	loss[2]	wins[3]	draws[3]	loses[3]
9	2	hard	hit	0.07	-	49.69	8.06	42.25
			DD	0.06	0.01	48.00	7.06	44.95
	3	hard	hit	0.10	0.02	51.16	7.80	41.04
			DD	0.12	-	49.59	6.83	43.58
	4	hard	hit	0.13	0.05	52.87	7.16	39.97
			DD	0.18	-	51.25	6.60	42.15
	5	hard	hit	0.16	0.08	54.45	6.91	38.64
			DD	0.24	-	52.89	6.37	40.74
	6	hard	hit	0.20	0.12	56.47	6.66	36.87
			DD	0.32	-	54.86	6.14	39.00
	7	hard	hit	0.17	-	53.48	10.23	36.29
			DD	0.10	0.07	49.15	6.92	43.93
	8	hard	hit	0.10	-	49.11	11.62	39.27
			DD	-0.03	0.13	45.22	8.24	46.54
	9	hard	hit	-0.05	-	38.89	16.99	44.11
			DD	-0.30	0.25	35.69	13.56	50.74
	10	hard	hit	-0.22	-	33.65	10.90	55.46
			DD	-0.58	0.36	31.50	7.77	60.73
	A	hard	hit	-0.35	-	27.53	9.62	62.85
			DD	-0.92	0.57	23.59	7.04	69.36

[1] *Mathematical expectation.*
[2] *Average cost of an incorrect decision, in bets lost per hand.*
[3] *Data in percentages, %.*

THE PLAYER HAS 8

With a total of 8 the player no longer finds himself in a favourable game situation (as with 9, 10 and 11). It is therefore never advantageous to double down and, consequently neither with inferior totals (many casinos do not even allow it).

This can be easily understood because, as we know, by doubling down we are entitled to receive one card and one card alone, so if when starting from a total of 8 we see that it is never advantageous to double down, consequently with lower starting totals, our chances of reaching a high total decrease even further and that will certainly not increase the advantage of doubling down.

4+4

The same goes for an 8 formed by 4+4, it is never convenient to divide the pair. The loss that the player would incur, or the cost of his error, is almost the same as if he were to double down.

PLAYER 8 - DEALER 2

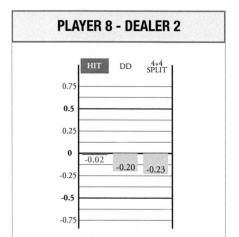

PLAYER 8 - DEALER 3

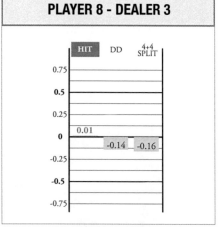

PLAYER 8 - DEALER 4

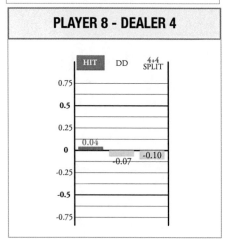

PLAYER 8 - DEALER 5

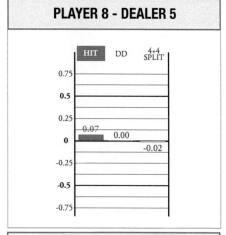

PLAYER 8 - DEALER 6

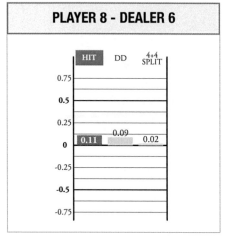

PLAYER 8 - DEALER 7

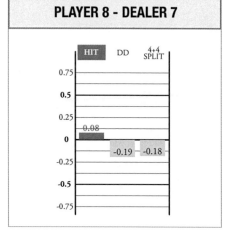

PLAYER 8 - DEALER 8

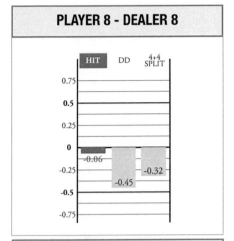

PLAYER 8 - DEALER 9

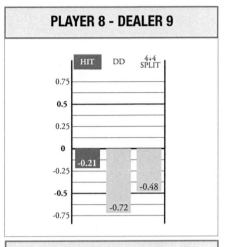

PLAYER 8 - DEALER 10

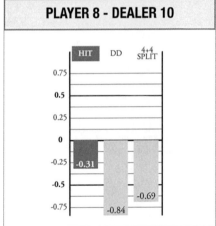

PLAYER 8 - DEALER A

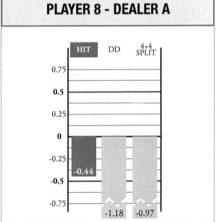

player	dealer	hand	decision	expectation[1]	loss[2]	wins[3]	draws[3]	loses[3]
8	2	hard	hit	-0.02	-	44.98	7.86	47.16
			DD	-0.20	0.18	41.77	6.22	52.00
		4+4	split	-0.23	0.21	17.78(x2)+3.48(x1)	45.45	28.82(x2)+4.43(x1)
	3	hard	hit	0.01	-	46.60	7.60	45.80
			DD	-0.14	0.15	43.57	6.02	50.41
		4+4	split	-0.16	0.17	19.26(x2)+3.50(x1)	45.91	27.17(x2)+4.15(x1)
	4	hard	hit	0.04	-	48.47	6.93	44.59
			DD	-0.07	0.11	45.43	5.81	48.75
		4+4	split	-0.10	0.14	21.07(x2)+3.00(x1)	46.77	25.83(x2)+3.33(x1)
	5	hard	hit	0.07	-	50.19	6.69	43.11
			DD	0.00	0.07	47.28	5.61	47.11
		4+4	split	-0.02	0.09	22.86(x2)+3.02(x1)	46.99	24.05(x2)+3.09(x1)
	6	hard	hit	0.11	-	52.55	6.40	41.05
			DD	0.09	0.02	49.50	5.36	45.14
		4+4	split	0.02	0.09	23.98(x2)+3.09(x1)	46.99	22.92(x2)+3.02(x1)
	7	hard	hit	0.08	-	48.23	11.76	40.01
			DD	-0.19	0.27	41.47	7.68	50.85
		4+4	split	-0.18	0.26	16.88(x2)+7.39(x1)	41.83	24.92(x2)+8.98(x1)
	8	hard	hit	-0.06	-	38.41	17.18	44.40
			DD	-0.45	0.39	32.18	13.03	54.78
		4+4	split	-0.32	0.26	13.96(x2)+6.97(x1)	40.71	28.41(x2)+9.94(x1)
	9	hard	hit	-0.21	-	33.68	11.62	54.70
			DD	-0.72	0.51	28.38	7.31	64.31
		4+4	split	-0.48	0.27	11.07(x2)+6.25(x1)	39.03	32.88(x2)+10.77(x1)
	10	hard	hit	-0.31	-	29.86	9.53	60.61
			DD	-0.84	0.53	26.35	5.14	68.50
		4+4	split	-0.69	0.38	8.10(x2)+4.91(x1)	36.56	39.58(x2)+10.85(x1)
	A	hard	hit	-0.44	-	23.12	9.34	67.54
			DD	-1.18	0.74	17.56	6.04	76.41
		4+4	split	-0.97	0.53	5.00(x2)+3.12(x1)	32.1	49.93(x2)+9.85(x1)

[1] *Mathematical expectation.*
[2] *Average cost of an incorrect decision, in bets lost per hand.*
[3] *Data in percentages, %.*

THE PLAYER HAS 7

A total of 7 can only be achieved with three combinations of cards: 2+5, 3+4 and 2+2+3. There is no alternative to hitting; standing makes no sense and neither does doubling down. The mathematical expectation remains negative.

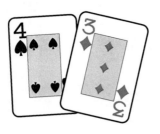

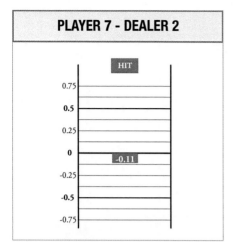

PLAYER 7 - DEALER 2

HIT

-0.11

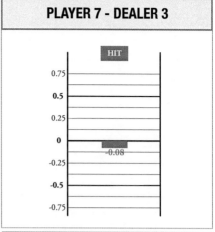

PLAYER 7 - DEALER 3

HIT

-0.08

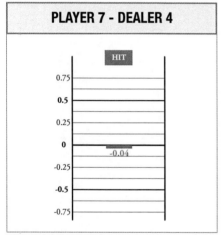

PLAYER 7 - DEALER 4

HIT

-0.04

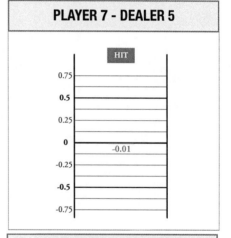

PLAYER 7 - DEALER 5

HIT

-0.01

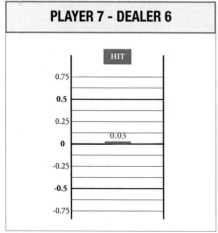

PLAYER 7 - DEALER 6

HIT

0.03

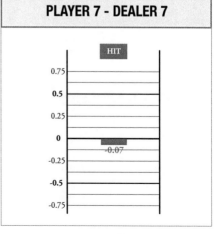

PLAYER 7 - DEALER 7

HIT

-0.07

PLAYER 7 - DEALER 8

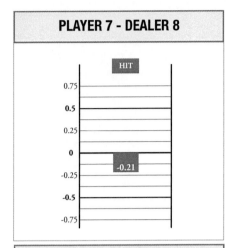

PLAYER 7 - DEALER 9

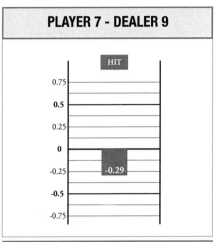

PLAYER 7 - DEALER 10

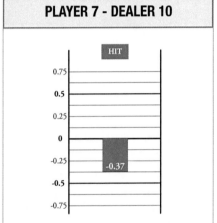

PLAYER 7 - DEALER A

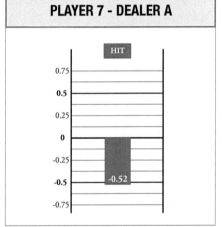

player	dealer	hand	decision	expectation[1]	loss[2]	wins[3]	draws[3]	loses[3]
7	2	hard	hit	-0.11	-	40.74	7.60	51.66
	3	hard	hit	-0.08	-	42.51	7.34	50.15
	4	hard	hit	-0.04	-	44.52	6.66	48.82
	5	hard	hit	-0.01	-	46.48	6.32	47.20
	6	hard	hit	0.03	-	47.73	7.46	44.81
	7	hard	hit	-0.07	-	37.93	17.27	44.81
	8	hard	hit	-0.21	-	33.59	11.76	54.65
	9	hard	hit	-0.29	-	30.64	10.18	59.18
	10	hard	hit	-0.37	-	26.68	9.46	63.86
	A	hard	hit	-0.52	-	19.48	8.80	71.72

[1] Mathematical expectation.
[2] Average cost of an incorrect decision, in bets lost per hand.
[3] Data in percentages, %.

THE PLAYER HAS 6

The player can obtain 6 only with 4+2 or 3+3.

In the first case, as seen for 7, he has no alternative but to hit, remaining with a negative mathematical expectation.

Not even if he starts the hand with a pair of 3's does the player find himself in a favourable game situation; however, in some cases, splitting the pair and playing two separate hands allows him to reduce the average loss. In particular against a 4, 5, 6 or 7. Against the 6 he even has an advantage over the dealer, with a mathematical expectation of +0.05.

.

PLAYER 6 - DEALER 2

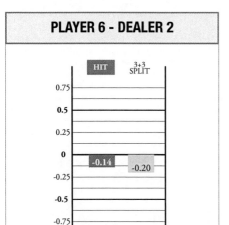

PLAYER 6 - DEALER 3

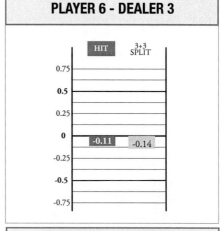

PLAYER 6 - DEALER 4

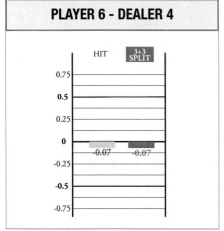

PLAYER 6 - DEALER 5

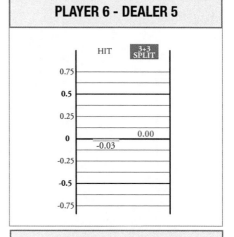

PLAYER 6 - DEALER 6

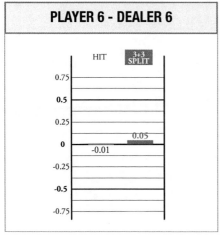

PLAYER 6 - DEALER 7

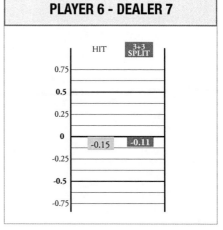

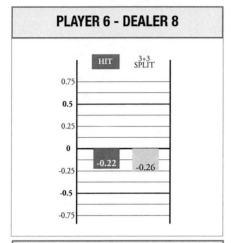

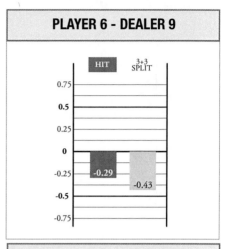

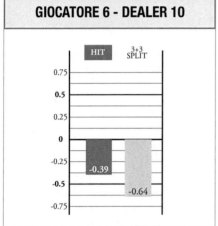

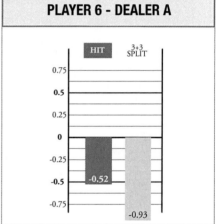

player	dealer	hand	decision	expectation[1]	loss[2]	wins[3]	draws[3]	loses[3]
6	2	hard	hit	-0.14	-	41.20	3.52	55.28
		3+3	split	-0.20	0.06	18.28(x2)+3.81(x1)	45.35	27.88(x2)+4.70(x1)
	3	hard	hit	-0.11	-	42.99	3.34	53.65
		3+3	split	-0.14	0.03	19.73(x2)+3.82(x1)	45.74	26.30(x2)+4.41(x1)
	4	hard	hit	-0.07	0.00	45.02	2.73	52.25
		3+3	split	-0.07	-	21.55(x2)+3.28(x1)	46.59	25.04(x2)+3.54(x1)
	5	hard	hit	-0.03	0.03	46.97	2.63	50.40
		3+3	split	0.00	-	23.34(x2)+3.29(x1)	46.77	23.31(x2)+3.29(x1)
	6	hard	hit	-0.01	0.06	47.90	2.79	49.31
		3+3	split	0.05	-	24.52(x2)+3.37(x1)	46.74	22.17(x2)+3.20(x1)
	7	hard	hit	-0.15	0.04	38.22	8.37	53.41
		3+3	split	-0.11	-	18.05(x2)+7.89(x1)	41.84	23.26(x2)+8.96(x1)
	8	hard	hit	-0.22	-	34.85	8.58	56.57
		3+3	split	-0.26	0.04	14.92(x2)+7.46(x1)	40.89	26.75(x2)+9.99(x1)
	9	hard	hit	-0.29	-	30.99	8.75	60.26
		3+3	split	-0.43	0.14	11.83(x2)+6.68(x1)	39.39	31.24(x2)+10.86(x1)
	10	hard	hit	-0.39	-	26.53	8.02	65.45
		3+3	split	-0.64	0.25	8.66(x2)+5.24(x1)	37.08	38.03(x2)+10.99(x1)
	A	hard	hit	-0.52	-	20.84	6.50	72.67
		3+3	split	-0.93	0.41	5.35(x2)+3.33(x1)	32.74	48.54(x2)+10.04(x1)

[1] *Mathematical expectation.*
[2] *Average cost of an incorrect decision, in bets lost per hand.*
[3] *Data in percentages, %.*

THE PLAYER HAS 5

The player can only have a total of 5 with 2+3.

There is no choice but to hit; standing makes no sense and neither does doubling down. The mathematical expectation remains in negative territory.

PLAYER 5 - DEALER 2

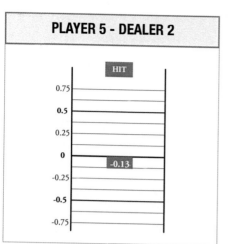

PLAYER 5 - DEALER 3

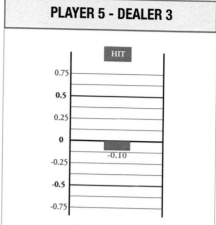

PLAYER 5 - DEALER 4

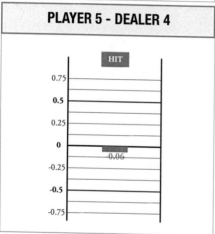

PLAYER 5 - DEALER 5

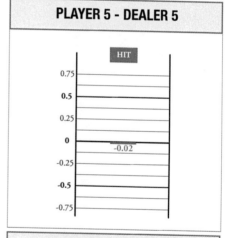

PLAYER 5 - DEALER 6

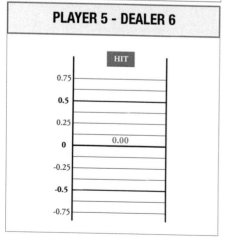

PLAYER 5 - DEALER 7

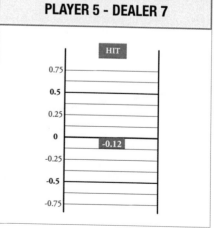

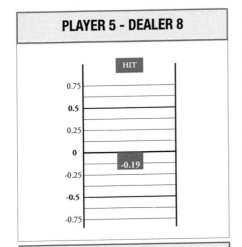

PLAYER 5 - DEALER 8

HIT

-0.19

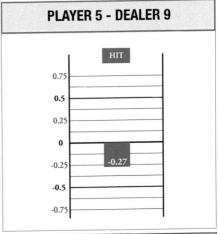

PLAYER 5 - DEALER 9

HIT

-0.27

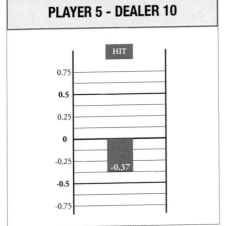

PLAYER 5 - DEALER 10

HIT

-0.37

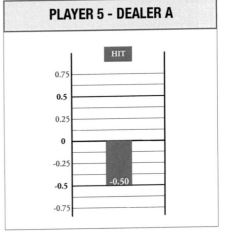

PLAYER 5 - DEALER A

HIT

-0.50

player	dealer	hand	decision	expectation[1]	loss[2]	wins[3]	draws[3]	loses[3]
5	2	hard	hit	-0.13	-	41.68	3.82	54.50
	3	hard	hit	-0.10	-	43.39	3.70	52.91
	4	hard	hit	-0.06	-	45.41	3.04	51.55
	5	hard	hit	-0.02	-	47.34	2.93	49.73
	6	hard	hit	0.00	-	48.48	2.91	48.61
	7	hard	hit	-0.12	-	39.68	8.69	51.63
	8	hard	hit	-0.19	-	36.09	9.01	54.90
	9	hard	hit	-0.27	-	32.14	9.07	58.80
	10	hard	hit	-0.37	-	27.50	8.32	64.18
	A	hard	hit	-0.50	-	21.60	6.73	71.66

[1] *Mathematical expectation.*
[2] *Average cost of an incorrect decision, in bets lost per hand.*
[3] *Data in percentages, %.*

THE PLAYER HAS 4

SPLIT WITH 2+2 AGAINST 4, 5, 6,

A total of 4 can only be obtained with 2+2 and the same rules apply as for a pair of 3's. With 2+2 we have two advantageous situations for the player that decides to split: against the dealer's 5 and 6 (expected gain between 0.03 and 0.08).

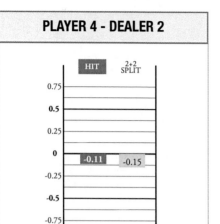

PLAYER 4 - DEALER 2

HIT: -0.11
2+2 SPLIT: -0.15

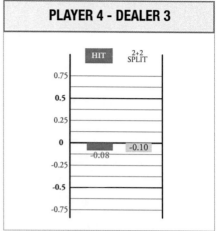

PLAYER 4 - DEALER 3

HIT: -0.08
2+2 SPLIT: -0.10

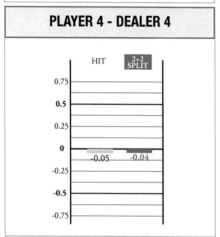

PLAYER 4 - DEALER 4

HIT: -0.05
2+2 SPLIT: -0.04

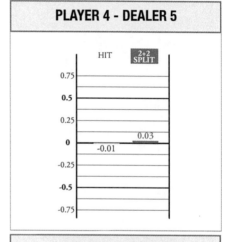

PLAYER 4 - DEALER 5

HIT: -0.01
2+2 SPLIT: 0.03

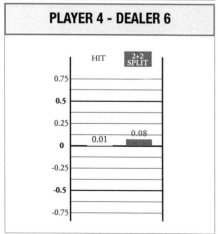

PLAYER 4 - DEALER 6

HIT: 0.01
2+2 SPLIT: 0.08

PLAYER 4 - DEALER 7

HIT: -0.09
2+2 SPLIT: -0.05

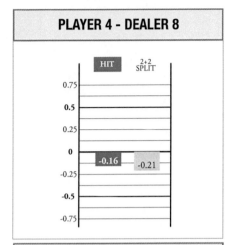

PLAYER 4 - DEALER 8

HIT   2+2 SPLIT

-0.16   -0.21

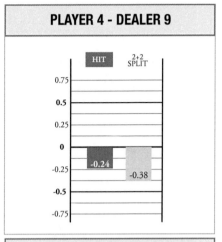

PLAYER 4 - DEALER 9

HIT   2+2 SPLIT

-0.24   -0.38

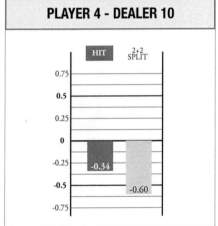

PLAYER 4 - DEALER 10

HIT   2+2 SPLIT

-0.34   -0.60

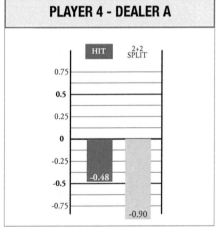

PLAYER 4 - DEALER A

HIT   2+2 SPLIT

-0.48   -0.90

player	dealer	hand	decision	expectation[1]	loss[2]	wins[3]	draws[3]	loses[3]
4	2	2+2	hit	-0.11	-	42.20	4.12	53.68
			split	-0.15	0.04	18.69(x2)+5.14(x1)	44.30	25.83(x2)+6.05(x1)
	3	2+2	hit	-0.08	-	43.90	3.97	52.13
			split	-0.10	0.02	19.94(x2)+5.13(x1)	44.63	24.61(x2)+5.70(x1)
	4	2+2	hit	-0.05	0.01	45.90	3.27	50.83
			split	-0.04	-	22.09(x2)+3.58(x1)	46.38	24.20(x2)+3.75(x1)
	5	2+2	hit	-0.01	0.04	47.82	3.15	49.04
			split	0.03	-	23.87(x2)+3.59(x1)	46.52	22.53(x2)+3.49(x1)
	6	2+2	hit	0.01	0.07	48.97	3.15	47.88
			split	0.08	-	25.10(x2)+3.68(x1)	46.46	21.37(x2)+3.39(x1)
	7	2+2	hit	-0.09	0.04	41.09	8.99	49.92
			split	-0.05	-	19.22(x2)+8.40(x1)	41.76	21.69(x2)+8.93(x1)
	8	2+2	hit	-0.16	-	37.37	9.33	53.30
			split	-0.21	0.05	15.89(x2)+7.95(x1)	40.99	25.17(x2)+10.00(x1)
	9	2+2	hit	-0.24	-	33.27	9.39	57.34
			split	-0.38	0.14	12.59(x2)+7.12(x1)	39.67	29.69(x2)+10.93(x1)
	10	2+2	hit	-0.34	-	28.47	8.62	62.91
			split	-0.60	0.26	9.21(x2)+5.59(x1)	37.54	36.54(x2)+11.12(x1)
	A	2+2	hit	-0.48	-	22.37	6.97	70.66
			split	-0.90	0.42	5.69(x2)+3.55(x1)	33.34	47.21(x2)+10.21(x1)

[1] *Mathematical expectation.*

[2] *Average cost of an incorrect decision, in bets lost per hand.*

[3] *Data in percentages, %.*

LOST

Sawyer and Hurley are on the beach playing Blackjack.

The backs of the cards bear the symbol of the Dharma Initiative, a hard suitcase provides the table and Sawyer is the dealer.

Hurley has the 2 of hearts and the K of clubs before him, Sawyer the 6 of diamonds and a down card.

Hurley: *Stick? I don't know, dude. Don't need 21? I think I should hit.*
Sawyer: *But I got a six. I'm gonna bust.*
Hurley: *How do you know that?*
Sawyer: *I don't. But you gotta assume that I'm gonna bust.*
Hurley: *Why?*

Sawyer shakes his head as if to say, "How on earth am I going to explain this?" and the scene fades out.

Lost references – and with a certain proficiency – a lot of games and Blackjack is no exception. We are in the second season, episode 12 "Fire + Water".

Well, try to answer Hurley's question and you will soon see that this is not just a random example; whoever scripted this episode understands Blackjack and purposefully chose a counterintuitive situation.
Hurley has a total of 12 and, being no expert, he wants to hit, as he is still a long way from 21; so he does not understand Sawyer's suggestion to stand. And one of the reasons is precisely Sawyer's exposed 6; when starting from a 6 the dealer has a high probability of going bust (42.32%), in

fact 6 is the first card with which the dealer has the greatest probability of going bust. That is why Hurley should stand, even with such a low total. To tell the truth we are in a borderline situation, the two choices are very close from the point of view of mathematical hope, -0.15 if he stands, -0.17 if he hits. So Hurley is at a disadvantage either way, but on average would lose a little bit less if he decided to stand.

Lost (TV series)
Season 2, episode 12 – *Fire + Water* (2005)
with Josh Halloway, Jorge Garcia

NUMB3RS

Numb3rs is a TV series based on the idea of using applied mathematics to solve apparently unsolvable police cases. FBI agent Don Eppes (Rob Morrow) therefore involves his brother Charlie (Krumholtz), a mathematics genius, in his investigations. Colleagues Larry Fleinhardt (Peter MacNicol) and Amita Ramanujan (Navi Rawat), a beautiful former student with whom Charlie is in a relationship, are often involved in the events, all set in Los Angeles.

In episode 13 of the second season, *Double Down*, our investigators find themselves tackling a homicide that took place in the car park of the Bicycle Casino.

The victim was a brilliant mathematics student who was part of a team for counting cards and winning at Blackjack. The references to *Blackjack Club* by Mezrich (see feature on 21) are almost too obvious, but it must be pointed out that this episode was aired two years before the film *21*, based on the novel by Mezrich, came out.

This time the star of the investigation is Charlie's colleague, Larry; it is Larry who realises that this is all connected to a team of counters, because he too was a counter when he was younger. He is not proud of his past, but is keen to explain that, far from the lure of easy winnings, he was motivated by the demonstration of the power of mathematics.

This intense episode underlines several times that card-counting isn't cheating, but just playing with intelligence, using precisely the power of mathematics that Larry talks about. Naturally the casino bosses do not share this

point of view and quite simply they will not tolerate losing money.

Thanks to Larry's specific knowledge, it emerges that the team did not stop at just counting cards, this time they were cheating for real. In fact they were financed by a consultant for the company that supplied Bicycle Casino with their card shuffling machines. They had made the machine's basic algorithm much simpler than it should have been and given it to the team, who were therefore able to predict, with some approximation, the order the cards would be dealt in (shuffle tracking). Science fiction? Maybe.

It should be noted that in the opening scene we see the future victim split a 20 against an 8. The basic strategy categorically excludes this split, but

naturally everything is much easier if you already know that another 10 and an Ace are on their way…

Trivia: in one of the scenes shot at the Bicycle the sound of a slot machine is heard in the background. But there's not a single slot machine at the Bicycle because it is not a real casino (there are no casinos in Los Angeles), but a card club, the biggest in the world for the record.

Numb3rs (TV series)
Season 2, episode 13 – *Double down* (2006)
with Rob Morrow, David Krumholtz, Peter MacNicol

LAS VEGAS

Las Vegas is a TV series of few pretensions; it is set in the Montecito Resort & Casino of Las Vegas, a fictional hotel-casino with cutting-edge technology and security. Naturally the residents and staff get involved in all sorts of problems, not to mention the many, for the most part fleeting, love affairs. The series really lifts the lid on the whole scene, exaggerating both its caprices and its vices.

Of course there had to be an episode about Blackjack card-counters. In *Double Down, Triple Threat*, the action kicks off with the unmasking of a counter by a sophisticated facial-recognition program.

Of course there's no love lost between the casinos and counters and in fact Ed Deline (James Caan), the director of Montecito, was on the point of reporting the culprit:

If we catch a card counter, we have to notify the Gaming Control. Then every casino in Nevada will be on the lookout for you. You see?

But at the last minute he realises that the counter is actually being blackmailed and decides to help him, along with loyal Danny McCoy (Josh Duhamel). The series is always garnished with the presence of attractive women and this episode is no exception.

Las Vegas (TV series)
Season 3, episode 3 – *Double down, triple threat* (2005)
with James Caan, Josh Duhamel

ADVANCED STRATEGY

Winner, winner, chicken dinner!

21 (film, 2008)
Ben Campbell (Jim Sturgess)

VARIABILITY

If the basic strategy is carefully followed, Blackjack is the most advantageous casino game for the player: the dealer's advantage is in fact reduced to a modest 0.7%, very little when compared to the 2.73% advantage he has in roulette.

To be more precise, this figure 0.07% refers to the game when it is played according to the rules that we accepted as the basic rules when writing this text, that is:
• It is played with 6 decks;
• No hole card rule;
• The dealer must stand on soft 17;
• No doubling down after a split, whereas splitting is permitted for any initial combination of cards;
• The pair can be re-split 4 times;
• Aces can only be split once.

But as we know, there are many variations to the rules and these obviously influence the dealer's advantage over the player.
In the following tables we show what percentage of advantage the player gains or loses through application of the different rules; the values shown must then be subtracted or added to -0.7 to obtain the player's real advantage.

RULE	PLAYER'S GAIN
1 deck	+0.57
2 decks	+0.22
4 decks	+0.07
8 decks	-0.07
Dealer hits with soft 17	-0.20
No doubling down with 9	-0.14
No doubling down with a soft hand	-0.14
No re-split	-0.06
Without No hole card	+0.13
Doubling down permitted after split	+0.14
Re-splitting Aces permitted	+0.07
Early surrender	+0.62
Late surrender	+0.06

The data is shown in percentages, %

If for example we assume that we are playing according to the rules most commonly used in the United States (4 decks, no double after split, dealer must stand on soft 17, doubling down permitted on any initial card, re-splitting allowed up to 4 times, Aces split only once, no "no hole card" rule), we can calculate that the dealer's advantage over the player is reduced to 0.5%.

So, small though it may be, the casino will always have a margin and in the long term this means it is always a winner.

But this game is different to all the rest; let's say that "the deck has a memory". This means that if the player can keep track of the cards that are dealt, he will be able to recognise points in the game where the casino's margin vanishes and even becomes favourable to the player. To best use this, the player must vary the value of his bets and make small adjustments to his strategy.

How is all this possible?

The answer lies in the rules of the game: the dealer is forced to hit with a total of 16 or less. When the deck is rich with high cards, it is more likely that the player will have a winning hand because the dealer, who is obliged to hit, has a higher probability of going bust.

The most important cards are the 10 and the Ace as they are the two cards that make blackjack (which wins a stake and a half) and therefore earn the most. Furthermore, in the calculations made to define the basic strategy, the hypothesis that the next card dealt will be worth 10 wields the greatest influence over individual probabilities. If you manage to keep track of the number of tens and Aces in the deck, you can find a way to turn the game to your favour.

Let's try to further understand these concepts with the help of mathematics.

Imagine playing with a single deck, artificially enhanced with extra tens: we remove four low cards (a 2, a 3, a 4 and a 5) and add 4 cards with a value of 10. Let's see how the probabilities of each card being dealt change:

REGULAR DECK		ENHANCED DECK	
A (4)	7.69	A (4)	7.69
2 (4)	7.69	2 (3)	5.77
3 (4)	7.69	3 (3)	5.77
4 (4)	7.69	4 (3)	5.77
5 (4)	7.69	5 (3)	5.77
6 (4)	7.69	6 (4)	7.69
7 (4)	7.69	7 (4)	7.69
8 (4)	7.69	8 (4)	7.69
9 (4)	7.69	9 (4)	7.69
10 (16)	30.77	10 (20)	38.46

The data is shown in percentages, %

We hypothesise that the dealer"s first card is a 6 and recalculate the distribution of probability with this new deck. The results are shown in this table, where the columns show the probability that the bank will close with the various totals starting from 6.

	17	18	19	20	21	>21
6 (enhanced)	15.18	8.62	8.81	8.67	8.54	50.19
6 (regular)	16.54	10.63	10.63	10.17	9.71	42.32

The data is shown in percentages, %

The difference compared to the regular deck is clear; all the percentages that the dealer will close with a certain total are decreased, while his percentage of going bust has increased.

Now let's assume that the player has a total of 14; the basic strategy tells us to stand, which means that our only chance of winning is that the dealer goes bust. So we're looking at:
• Probability of winning: 50.19%
• Probability of drawing: 0%
• Probability of losing: 49:81%

Whereas with a normal deck we're looking at:
• Probability of winning: 42.32%
• Probability of drawing: 0%
• Probability of losing: 57.68%

It is clear that in this particular situation, with a deck enhanced with extra 10s, the player is in a more advantageous position. In fact he has a 7.87% higher chance of beating the dealer and whereas normally he would be in a disadvantaged position with a mathematical hope equal to -0.15, this abundance of 10s means his mathematical hope is close to 0.

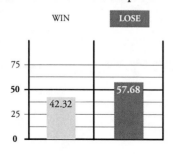

Normal deck

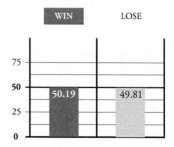

Enhanced deck

The artificial example outlined here clearly demonstrates how a deck with extra 10s gives the player an advantage. And this is also true in real situations: the more 10s in the deck, the greater advantage the player has. (Don't worry; we'll just accept it's proven to avoid boring you with every single calculation!)

It follows that if a player were able to keep count of all the cards dealt, he would be able to recognise the moments when the deck had more 10s in it than usual and decide to bet more precisely to exploit those especially favourable moments.

CARD-COUNTING METHODS

There are numerous methods for card-counting, but the basic idea remains the same for them all: knowing how many 10s and Aces are present in the remaining deck.

What is more, every different method is structured in the same way; in fact they are based on five concepts:

1) *Basic strategy*. If you want to count cards the first thing is to be able to use the basic strategy and all its variants perfectly.

2) *Running count*. Different values are assigned to each card (positive for low cards and negative for high cards) and you remember only the running total given by the sum of the values of all the cards that are dealt face-up from the deck. If the total is negative the deck has few high cards and is therefore favourable to the dealer. The value to assign to each card varies according to the method used. In any case the total is zero when the deck is new or has just been shuffled.

3) *True count*. Convert the running count into a true count, or rather a number that does not just take into account the dealt cards, but also how much of the deck has been used. It is obvious that a positive value has much less value at the beginning of the deck than when it has already been largely used.

4) *Basic strategy variations*. In some situations, on the basis of the true count, you should deviate from the basic strategy, as it is more advantageous to make a different decision.

5) *Bet*. Here we draw on the consequences of all the previous calculations, use the opportunity to vary the bet: bet more when the deck is favourable and less when it is unfavourable.

THE HIGH-LOW METHOD

The most famous and simplest card-counting method is called High-Low, it was proposed for the first time by Harvey Dubner at the Fall Joint Computer Conference in Las Vegas in 1963. Braun then took the idea and perfected it with the aid of fast computers and this is the method that would appear in the second edition of *Beat the Dealer*, in 1966.

In general, this is the method referred to when discussing the card-counting methods, it is the most widely used as it is simple to learn and yet provides an opportunity to gain a real advantage over the dealer.

Further advantage can be gained with other methods, compensated for however by the increased complexity of the methods themselves and the consequent risks of making mistakes in the counting.

The High-Low method is therefore without a doubt the best compromise. It owes its name to the fact that all you need to do is simply add or subtract 1 from the count depending on whether the card dealt is low or high.

The table shows which value to attribute to each card.

CARD	VALUE
2	+1
3	+1
4	+1
5	+1
6	+1
7	0
8	0
9	0
10	-1
J	-1
Q	-1
K	-1
A	-1

When a new deck is started or reshuffled our count goes back to zero and, for every card dealt during the game, we simply have to update our count by following the table.

Let us assume for example, that, starting from a new or reshuffled deck, the cards turned over are the following:

SEQUENCE OF CARDS TURNED OVER											
2	5	4	10	7	J	K	8	A	6	J	8
VALUE OF EACH CARD USING THE HIGH-LOW METHOD											
1	1	1	-1	0	-1	-1	0	-1	1	-1	0
RUNNING COUNT											
1	2	3	2	2	1	0	0	-1	0	-1	-1

As you can see there's nothing complicated about it, you don't need to be a maths genius to count cards, with practice and training it is entirely possible to become skilled counters.

The next step is to move on from the running count to the true count. With the total calculated we know how many high cards there are in the deck in comparison to the low cards present, but it is not an absolute count. If, for example, the total is +5 it simply means that there are 5 less low cards than high cards. However these 5 cards might have been the first 5 cards the dealer dealt or perhaps 30 low cards have been dealt and only 25 high cards, and there is a huge difference between the two cases. What we are really interested in is how probable it is that the next card will be a high card, clearly this gradually increases as more of the deck is used. In other words, the higher the number of cards dealt, the more valuable the totals become.

Let us calculate for example the probability of a 10 or an Ace being dealt in the following two cases, both with a calculated total of +8:

case a) The 6 decks have just been reshuffled and each of the 8 first cards dealt were low. There are 304 cards left (52x6-8), 96 of which are 10s or Aces (all those contained in 6 decks); the probability of a 10 or Ace being dealt is therefore 96/304=31.6% (against 30.8% of the uncut deck).

case b) Only 2 out of the 6 decks remain. The calculation is more approximative here; 104 cards remain and there are 8 more high cards than low cards. Let us assume that the number of neutral cards (7, 8 and 9) is in line with the number of decks, therefore 3x4x2=24. There will therefore be an average of 44 high cards and 36 low cards and the probability of a 10 or Ace being dealt is 44/104=42.3%.

As you can see, there is a huge difference.

In order to be as precise as possible, it is recommended that you also take half decks into consideration. If for example our count is +24 and only two and a half decks remain, the true count would be 24/2.5=9.6.

Working out the number of decks left to play is simpler than it seems, because the casino always keep the used cards in sight so as to demonstrate that they are not cheating.

The shoe is constructed in such a way that it is easy for the dealer to extract one card at a time without showing the next cards, and the cards are placed horizontally making it difficult to work out how many cards remain; the pile of used cards on the other hand is placed vertically and in sight of all the players (actually some positions at the table are preferable, because they give a clear view of the pile of used cards without attracting attention). All we need to do then is to learn how to assess the deck of used cards to establish how many cards remain in the shoe. If we are playing with 6 decks and we calculate that there are 2 decks in the pile of used cards, 4 decks must remain in the shoe.

HOW TO VARY YOUR BETS

The concept is simple: bet more when the true count is high and less when it is low.

It is all a matter of finding the most efficient method for converting the true count into the sum of the bet itself. Many different systems exist, some of which are very complex, but we have chosen the method that we will go on to explain for its simplicity. It is a method that on the one hand allows you to make the most of the information gained from counting the cards and on the other is not very difficult.

The dealer starts off with an advantage of approximately 0.7% (using our basic rules), after which the true count and advantage/disadvantage vary in direct proportion: it can be estimated that every time the true count is increased by +1 the player's advantage increases by approximately 0.5%.

The following diagram shows the pattern of the true count (TC) on the x-axis in proportion to the player's advantage/disadvantage.

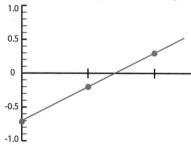

By using different game rules, the dealer's initial advantage varies (with the consequent vertical translation of the line), but the pattern remains the same.

The diagram instantly shows that with a positive total of just over 1, the player is equal with the dealer (something that does not happen in any other casino games). Then with a count of +2 the player takes the advantage with a margin of 0.3%: the roles are reversed and it's time to make the most of the situation!

A good strategy has to ensure that the amount of money bet increases as the player's advantage increases. This can be done by using the true count, as it is proportional to the advantage, as a sort of multiplier in order to determine the optimum bet. Let's see how…

1) First of all you need to choose a basic bet. This basic unit will be the minimum amount that you bet every time the count is not favourable and its amount depends entirely on the player's bankroll (the bankroll is the total amount of money that we have decided to play with); it is completely independent of the method, the method functions in the same way no matter what the basic unit is. We will work with a basic bet of 1.

2) Then we adjust the true count by subtracting 1 for every 0.5% of initial advantage for the casino; in our case (advantage 0.7%) we will approximate, subtracting 1.5. In America (advantage 0.5%), we would have subtracted 1. If for example the count is +3, the adjusted count will be 3-1.5=1.5.

3) We multiply the adjusted true count by the basic bet. Every time the total is equal to or less than 1, we will continue to bet the basic bet; but if the product is greater than 1, we bet that amount instead.

Esempio 1
True count = +2
Product 1x(2-1.5) = 0.5
Bet = 1 (because the product is <1)

Esempio 2
True count = +4.5
Product 1x(4.5-1.5) = 3
Bet = 3

THE KELLY CRITERION

This formula, discovered by Professor J.L Kelly in 1956 and published in the *Bell System Technical Journal*, determines the optimum dimension of a series of bets and allows players to maximise their earnings in the long term by minimising risks. It has been mathematically proven and is relevant to all games of chance but was first applied to Blackjack by E. Thorp in his *Beat the Dealer*. The general form is as follows:

$$f = \frac{bp\text{-}q}{b}$$

Where:

f is the fraction of our bankroll that we will bet
b represents how much our bet pays out (b to 1)
p is the probability of victory
q is the probability of defeat

If applied to Blackjack, the Kelly formula tells us to bet a percentage of our overall bankroll that is equal to the advantage the dealer has at that particular moment. All we need to know is the casino's basic advantage (BA) and the true count (since we know that any every increase of a counting unit of 1 corresponds to an advantage for the player of 0.5). The player's total advantage, which corresponds to the fraction (*f*) of the bankroll to bet, is therefore:

$$f = \text{-}VB\text{+}0.5xTC$$

Let us re-examine the examples seen above:

E.g. 1) True count: +2
        Percentage of the bankroll to bet = -0.7+0.5x2 = 0.3%
        Bankroll = 1000 euros
        Bet = 3 euros

E.g. 2) True count = +4
        Percentage of the bankroll to bet = 0.7+0.5x4 = 1.3%
        Bankroll = 1000 euros
        Bet = 13 euros

The Kelly Criterion does not differ greatly from the method explained above; it is just fundamental for keeping track of our advantage over the casino and betting accordingly.

HOW TO VARY THE STRATEGY

Now we are able to work out when the deck is in favour of the player and vary our bets accordingly; this alone gives us a good advantage over the dealer. However, we can obtain an even greater advantage by modifying, in certain cases, the basic strategy, in keeping with the information obtained by counting the cards.

What we need to do is exploiting the fact that the probability of the next card being a 10 or an Ace varies as the count changes.

The hypothesis of the infinite deck used to calculate the basic strategy cannot always be used when the count exceeds certain values, or rather when the density of 10s and Aces deviates too much from the usual amount in an uncut deck. This is because in Blackjack the deck has a memory, or in other words the cards that have been dealt influence the outcome of the subsequent hits. If proportionally more 10s than normal or less 10s than normal are dealt, at certain levels the deck ceases to be a theoretically infinite object and becomes real. Its composition deviates slightly from the standard and it is therefore possible that the basic strategy varies as a consequence. Precisely what happens is clearly shown in the example of the enriched deck that we described above.

For example, there may be situations when with a low count (a deck lacking in 10s), it might be preferable to hit rather than stand; and vice versa in other situations with a high count (a deck with a lot of 10s) it will be convenient to split a pair that under normal circumstances we would not divide.

Deviating from the basic strategy is only important in a few cases, situations that recur with a certain frequency as changes are made to the strategy when there is a low count. In most cases the basic strategy remains unchanged, or rather, it is only changed when the true count is very high or very low and either way the advantage to be gained is so modest that it is not worth worrying about. There are in reality boundary numbers for practically every possible hand, but the majority of these game situations happen extremely rarely and do not actually obtain a significant advantage.

In 1986 Don Schlesinger simulated the "boundary numbers" for most possible situations, meaning that for each of these he checked at which value of the real calculation it would make sense to modify the basic strategy. Thus he showed that only in a handful of cases is it worth memorising the variations, and he called these cases Illustrious 18 and Fab 4. Let's examine these important cases.

Illustrious 18

TRUE COUNT	PLAYER	DEALER	BASIC STRATEGY	VARIATION
≥+3	Any total	A	No insurance	Insurance
≥ 0	16	10	Hit	Stand
≥+5	16	9	Hit	Stand
≥+4	15	10	Hit	Stand
≤-1	13	2	Stand	Hit
≤-2	13	3	Stand	Hit
≥+3	12	2	Hit	Stand
≥+2	12	3	Hit	Stand
< 0	12	4	Stand	Hit
≤-2	12	5	Stand	Hit
≤-1	12	6	Stand	Hit
≥+1	11	A	Hit	Double down
≥+4	10	A	Hit	Double down
≥+4	10	10	Hit	Double down
≥+3	9	7	Hit	Double down
≥+1	9	2	Hit	Double down
≥+4	10+10	6	Stand	Split
≥+5	10+10	5	Stand	Split

Let's look at this table together.

The first case can be read like this: "If the true count is greater than or equal to 3 and the dealer has an Ace, the player should take insurance, whatever his hand." The reasoning is clear, I insure myself against the possibility that the dealer gets a 10… but at this point the deck is full of 10s!

The second case: "If the true count is greater than or equal to 0 and the player has 16 and the dealer 10, the player should stand instead of hitting." This case occurs relatively frequently, as all that is required is that the true count is not negative. It is a particular case and in fact even in the basic strategy the options of standing or hitting have practically identical mathematical hope.

The third case: "If the true count is greater than or equal to 5 and the player has 16 and the dealer has 9, the player should stand instead of hitting." And so on.

Fab 4

TRUE COUNT	PLAYER	DEALER	SURRENDER
< 0	15	10	NO
≥+1	15	A	YES
≥+2	15	9	YES
≥+3	14	10	YES

The Fabulous 4 refer to strategy variations to the late surrender, where this is permitted. Whereas normally with 15 against 10 we should ask to surrender, we do not do so if the true count is negative and, what is more, we can see from the table that there are three other cases in which it becomes advantageous to surrender.

In the following tables we show our basic strategy; the fields containing numbers represent variations to the strategy (only the most important, that is, the Illustrious 18 listed above).

STAND/HIT TABLE: strategy variations

	2	3	4	5	6	7	8	9	10	A
12	3	2	0	-2	-1					
13	-1	-2								
14										
15									4	
16								5	0	
17										

▮ Stand
▯ Hit

In the fields marked stand, the cases where our basic strategy recommends that we stand, we should vary the strategy and therefore hit if the true count is less than or equal to the number displayed. In the fields marked hit we should instead vary the strategy if the true count is greater than or equal to the boundary number.

DOUBLE DOWN AND SPLIT TABLE: strategy variations

	2	3	4	5	6	7	8	9	10	A
9	1					3				
10									4	4
11										1
10+10				5	4					

▮ Stand
▯ Hit
▮ Double down

This table tells us to split or double down, where we would not normally do so, when the true count is greater than or equal to the number displayed; when it is less than the number displayed we follow the strategy.

An example calculation: player 12 – dealer 4

We have seen the most important variations to the basic strategy after counting the cards. Now let's try to understand the reasoning for these variations by doing the complete calculations for one of them: player 12 – bank 4.

Obviously 12 is not a good hand for the player, in fact the mathematical hope is highly negative. However, it is a hand that card-counting can significantly influence. The basic strategy tells us to stand against the dealer's 4.

But things change if the count is negative, let's have a look.

We hypothesise that we are playing this hand (12 vs. 4) when 51 cards remain in the shoe, exactly corresponding to a whole single deck minus one card (10), leaving 4 Aces, four 2s, four 3s and so on until 15 10s (as opposed to 16). The running total is -1, because there is one 10 less than the average, and the true count is also -1, as there is only 1 deck left before the shoe runs out. Each card will therefore have the following probabilities of being dealt:

CARD	QUANTITY	PROBABILITY
A	4	7.84
2	4	7.84
3	4	7.84
4	4	7.84
5	4	7.84
6	4	7.84
7	4	7.84
8	4	7.84
9	4	7.84
10	15	29.41

The data is shown in percentages, %

If we then recalculate the distribution of the dealer's probability from a 4 we obtain the following results:

DEALER: 4	17	18	19	20	21	>21
Deck without a 10 *True count -1*	13.24	12.77	12.31	11.81	11.28	38.61
Complete deck *true count 0*	13.05	12.59	12.41	11.65	11.12	39.45

The data is shown in percentages, %

Now let's see how these small variations influence the player's decisions.

With a complete deck (true count 0) we have:

	STAND	HIT
WIN	39.45%	36.99%
DRAW	0%	4.66%
LOSE	60.55%	58.35%
MATHEMATICAL HOPE	-0.211	-0.213

Therefore, if exactly one deck of 52 cards were missing (true count 0), it would be advantageous to stand, even if by very little.

Whereas with the deck missing a 10 (true count -1) we would have:

	STAND	HIT
WIN	38.61%	38.46%
DRAW	0%	4.82%
LOSE	61.41%	56.72%
MATHEMATICAL HOPE	-0.23	-0.18

In this case, with a negative true count (-1) it is clearly advantageous to hit. It remains nevertheless difficult to win, but the possibility of drawing increases and therefore the hope is less negative.

AN OUTLINE OF MORE COMPLICATED METHODS

As we have already mentioned there are numerous card-counting methods studied by mathematicians and expert players in order to increase the players' advantage over the casino (or to sell books).

There are two main characteristics that distinguish a card-counting method and make it different from the others:

• The <u>level</u>, which depends on the value assigned to the individual cards. For example the high-low method is level 1 (the values are +1, 0 and -1), a method in which the values assigned are +2 or -2 is second level and so on.

• Whether it is <u>balanced</u> or not, meaning whether the total sum of the points of all the cards in the deck is equal to zero.

We chose to explain the high-low method because, while being extremely simple, it obtains a concrete advantage; now let's have a quick look at some of the other methods.

Obviously as well as the different values assigned to each card, the boundary numbers that lead us to vary the strategy are different as well.

Level 1 – Hi-opt I

This first level method keeps track of the number of cards from 3 to 6 in comparison to the 10s. Therefore, unlike the high-low method, 2 is attributed a value of zero, as is the Ace:

CARD	VALUE
2	0
3	+1
4	+1
5	+1
6	+1
7	0
8	0
9	0
10	-1
J	-1
Q	-1
K	-1
A	0

We see that the system remains balanced; here too we have to divide our count by the number of remaining decks to obtain the true count that will enable us to decide how much to bet.

Level 2 – Hi–opt II

This system is much more complicated than its level 1 brother and is only used by great professionals; in any case the advantage obtained is extremely low and the game's not worth the candle.

Its difficulty stems from the fact that the values of the cards vary and it becomes harder to keep track without making mistakes. This table show the value that is attributed to each card:

CARD	VALUE
2	+1
3	+1
4	+2
5	+2
6	+1
7	+1
8	0
9	0
10	-2
J	-2
Q	-2
K	-2
A	0

Level 3 – Uston APC

This is one of the most powerful methods, but also the most complicated, developed by Kenneth Uston, one of the best Blackjack players in history. Here again the table shows the values assigned to each card, this is a level 3 method so some cards have values up to +/- 3.

CARD	VALUE
2	+1
3	+2
4	+2
5	+3
6	+2
7	+2
8	+1
9	-1
10	-3
J	-3
Q	-3
K	-3
A	0

As usual, the running count is converted into the true count, which gives us a precise indication of the composition of the remaining decks. Unlike other methods, in order to obtain the true count in this case we have to divide the running count by the number of half-decks remaining, rather than the number of decks. So if 1 and a half decks remain to play, our divisor will no longer be 1.5 but 3.

Counting the Aces

Some methods can be improved on by keeping count of the Aces separately, in particular those methods where the Ace is assigned a value of 0. There are various methods for monitoring how many Aces have been dealt without having to keep track of another number: we might use the chips for example, or the position of our feet.

Once we know how many Aces have been dealt and the number of cards that remain in play, we can easily estimate if less Aces than average have been dealt, meaning that our deck contains plenty of Aces, or if we've seen a number greater than the average then we know that our deck contains few Aces.

For every extra Ace in the deck we add to our running count (+1 if it's a first level method, +2 if it's a second level method, etc.), for every Ace less than the average on the other hand, we subtract the same value.

Knowing whether there are more or less Aces in the deck influences our betting strategy more than the game strategy, this additional calculation is only made to help decide how much to bet and players must return to the original running count to decide how to play.

Unbalanced - KO method

Also known as the Knock-Out system, the KO method is the most famous unbalanced card-counting method, explained in detail in the book *Knock-Out Blackjack*, by Olaf Vancura and Ken Fuchs. The difference compared to the High-Low method is that 7 is also considered a low card, as shown in the table below:

CARD	VALUE
2	+1
3	+1
4	+1
5	+1
6	+1
7	+1
8	0
9	0
10	-1
J	-1
Q	-1
K	-1
A	-1

This unbalanced method does not require the conversion of the running count into the true count.

COUNTERMEASURES

Over the years the casinos have adopted different new rules in an attempt to limit their losses, which are as follows:

• Shuffling the deck after every hand played (a rule also applied in most online casinos), or at least very frequently, perhaps using automatic shuffling machines;
• Cutting the deck so that only a small part is used before shuffling;
• Reducing the range of possible bets between the minimum and maximum so that card-counters can only exploit favourable situations to a limited extent.

Despite this, card-counting methods continue to work, as not all casinos have adopted these countermeasures. Perhaps you are asking yourself why not if it would limit their losses?

The fact is that frequent shuffling means playing less hands, and this is a loss for the casinos, as is lowering the maximum bets. Less money spent means less money earned, all in a bid to stop the tiny percentage of players who are capable of beating the game: it's not worth it!

Furthermore, automatic shuffling machines are expensive and often players do not trust them.

RAIN MAN

When his father dies, Charlie Babbit (Tom Cruise) discovers he has an autistic older brother, Raymond (Dustin Hoffman), who lives in an institution and is due to inherit the entirety of his father's fortune. Charlie feels cheated and is initially furious, especially considering his pressing financial needs. He takes his autistic brother away without really realising the extent of his problems and his need to strictly adhere to a long series of daily routines. So, in true American style, the brothers start out on a road trip and as time goes on succeed in establishing a connection. Memories surface of a distant past in which it was actually Charlie who mispronounced Raymond's name as Rain Man, which became his nickname. Charlie then discovers that alongside the problems typically linked to autism, Raymond also has some superhuman capabilities: an incredible ability for calculations and a formidable memory. He is in fact a "savant"; he possesses incredible islands of brilliant ability that are in extreme contrast with his general mental disability.

As they pass through Las Vegas Charlie is struck with an idea: it would be

a piece of cake for Raymond to count cards at Blackjack (even without understanding what he was doing) and that way Charlie could win at the casino. And in fact he does win a large and, for him, extremely useful amount, but there's no love between the casino and counters; security realises that something is amiss at that table and the pair are given the chance to keep their winnings and never show their faces again. Charlie has enough sense to accept.

The two brothers finally arrive at Los Angeles, Charlie wants to gain custody of his brother, but at the hearing he realises he would not be able to give him the attention he needs.

An excellent performance by Dustin Hoffman, who represents Raymond's complex interior world with great sensitivity: he won the Academy Award for best actor. The film won another three Academy Awards, one of which went to Barry Morrow for best screenplay.

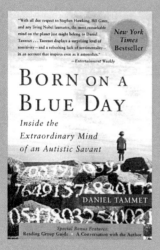

Few people are aware that Raymond's character was not fictional, but came from Barry Morrow's encounter with Kim Peek, a true savant. Kim's story is touchingly told by Daniel Tammet, the first savant who was able to describe his life and, above all, his sensations. He is in fact the author of the 2006 book *Born on a Blue Day*. Tammet, who has met Kim personally, recounts how, "In 1984 Kim and his father met producer and screenwriter Barry Morrow at a conference of the association of Retarded Citizens of Arlington in Texas. The result of that encounter was Rain Man. Dustin Hoffman spent a day with Kim and was so struck by his ability that he urged Fran [Kim's father ed.] to share his son's experience with the rest of the world. Since then, Kim and his father have toured far and wide across the United States, speaking to over a million people".

Rain Man (1988)
by Barry Levinson
with Dustin Hoffman, Tom Cruise, Valeria Golino

21 / BLACKJACK CLUB

Boston, MIT, Professor Micky Rosa's mathematics class.

Micky: *All right, now, let's give Ben a chance for some extra credit, shall we? We're gonna call this the game show host problem, all right? Ben, suppose you're on a game show. And you are given a chance to choose from three different doors, all right? Now, behind one of the doors is a new car. Behind the other two, goats. Which door would you choose, Ben?*

Ben: *Door number one?*

Micky: *Door number one. Ben chooses door number one. All right, now, the game show host, who, by the way, knows what's behind all the other doors, decides to open another door. Let's say he chooses door number three. Behind which sits a goat. Now...Ben, game show host comes up to you. He says, "Ben, do you want to stay with door number one "or go with door number two?" Now, is it in your interest to switch your choice?*

Ben: *Yeah.*

Micky: *Well, wait. Remember, the host knows where the car is so how do you know he's not playing a trick on you? Trying to use reverse psychology to get you to pick a goat?*

Ben: *Well, I wouldn't really care. I mean, my answer's based on statistics. Based on variable change.*

Micky: *Variable change? But he just asked you a simple question.*

Ben: *Yeah, which changed everything.*

Micky: *Enlighten us.*

Ben: *Well, when I was originally asked to choose a door, I had a 33.3% chance of choosing right. But after he opens one of the doors and then re-offers me the choice, it's now 66.7% if I choose to switch. So, yeah, I'll take door*

number two and thank you for that extra 33.3%.

Micky: *Exactly. People, remember, if you don't know which door to open, always account for variable change. Now, see, most people wouldn't take the switch out of paranoia, fear, emotions. But Mr Campbell, he kept emotions aside and let simple math get his ass into a brand-new car! Which is better than that goat you've been driving around campus.*

This problem is known as the *Monty Hall puzzle*, because in the Seventies there was actually a television programme called *Let's Make a Deal,* and it was of course presented by Monty Hall. It is by virtue of his brilliant response that Micky decides to recruit Ben for his Blackjack Team, a group of mathematics students who plan to beat the Las Vegas casinos by playing Blackjack.

It's a game with memory. Cards drawn are the past, ones to come are future. And the best part, it's beatable.

The trick to winning is playing in a team; the spotters sit at tables, playing the minimum and keeping count of the cards. When the count is advantageous they make a signal to the "big players", who bet high and generally win. But it's not easy, you need talent and discipline.

Listen, you not only have a gifted mind, but you're also composed. You don't give in to your emotions. You think logically. Ben, you were born for this. You'll have more fun than you've ever had in your entire life. It's perfect.

And so begins an extraordinary journey. Trips to Las Vegas, money, luxury and entertainment. But although card-counting is not illegal and cannot be considered cheating, the casinos certainly do not approve of it and have no qualms in taking the appropriate countermeasures. The fairly predictable plot evolves from here.

BEN
MEZRICH

Blackjack Club

La vera storia dei sei studenti di matematica
che hanno sbancato Las Vegas

STRADE
BLU

SAGGI
MONDADORI

Despite being panned by the critics, the film enjoyed great success at the box office. It is after all an enjoyable film to watch, thanks too to the ever great Kevin Spacey (Micky Rosa) and Laurence Fishburne (Cole Williams, the determined head of security at the casino). The one thing that is completely unfathomable is why they always played in the same casino, knowing full well that the security team was suspicious of them.

The film tells the shortened, watered-down version of the real "Blackjack Team" from Boston MIT, as told in the bestselling *Bringing Down the House* by Ben Mezrich. *Bringing Down the House* is impossible to put down as a novel and stuffed with cliff-hangers, but is actually a fairly accurate reconstruction of the real events, based on the testimony of one of the team members.

21 (2008)
by Robert Luketich
with Kevin Spacey, Laurence Fishburne, Jim Sturgess

Bringing Down the House (2002)
by Ben Mezrich
Free Press

PLAYING ONLINE

*One should always play fair
when one has the winning cards.*

Oscar Wilde

*I love blackjack. But I'm not addicted to gambling.
I'm addicted to sitting in a semi circle.*

Mitch Hedberg

This chapter was written in collaboration with the editorial office of *Jokonline*

ONLINE BLACKJACK VARIANTS

Blackjack solitaire

This is the most classic formula, used not only for Blackjack but also for many other games offered online. In short each player plays against the computer (which acts as the dealer), on a private table with no other players. It is essentially an individual game that the system then compares against other individual games completed by other competitors, with no direct match.

Once the entry fee has been paid, the game screen opens and players are assigned starting chips. Once the set number of hands has been played (from 10 to 25 depending on the site), a score is calculated based on the number of chips each participant has, the number of hands won against the dealer and any bonuses earned for saved time. The obvious limitation of this formula is that players have no way of knowing what their opponent (or opponents) is doing; this opponent might be playing his own game either simultaneously or at a separate time. It is an on-demand game as it were, where it is impossible (with the exception of the progressive Jackpot) to know how the tournament is progressing until the final results are displayed.

Game strategy should be based on speed and chip management… but unfortunately this cannot be applied, as we cannot see our opponents' stack or bets.

There is also a new factor to be taken into consideration: time. There is a limit on the time available to make your bets and it is generally very short: you cannot be distracted, you cannot play calmly and your decisions must be made pretty much instantly. Just like a videogame. If the time runs out any bets that haven't

been made cannot be finished; but to compensate, there are extra points if you finish within the allocated time.

There are different types of solitary tournament depending on the concessionaire and even within the same concessionaire:

Progressive jackpot. this is an individual game where the player seeks to get the highest score possible. The tournament lasts a certain number of hours or even a couple of days. During that period you can play as many games as you'd like in an attempt to improve your result. When gaming is closed, prizes are awarded to the players with the highest scores. The sum of prizes and number of players who receive them obviously depends on the number of participants: the jackpot is higher the more players there are. In some cases there is a guaranteed minimum, regardless of the number of players.

Head to head. by contrast head to head tournaments are always open. You play your game and, when one or more opponents have participated in the same tournament, the final classification is drawn up. This gaming method involves a limited number of players – usually from 2 to 5 – and awards prizes based on the number of participants and the total sum of the entry fee. The choice of name is curious as it implies a competition between two individual players but this is not the case.

Countdown. this type of tournament has a set number of players; each plays a game and once finished the classification is drawn up on the basis of each player's score. In practice it is very similar to the head to head games, but here players know how many other people have already played (although they do not know their scores) and how many still have to play.

Lobby blackjack

In this type of tournament players sit at a table alongside other players who play in the flesh at the same time, just like in poker. Everybody starts with the same amount of chips, the game is played over several hands and the winner is decided on the basis of the final classification and not individual hands. Thankfully in this game there is no time limit hanging over players like the sword of Damocles, but decisions are nevertheless made in real time: players have just seconds to decide, much like in a poker tournament. In addition to keeping track of the normal basic strategy, in this type of game it is fundamental to choose how much to bet based on what your opponents do. And this is the beauty of playing Blackjack against other players and not against the dealer. It is not just a matter of the mechanical decision of what to do when comparing your cards against the dealer, but also, and especially, deciding how much to bet mainly on the basis of the opponents' stacks. Playing the opponent, and not just the dealer, is like introducing typical game thinking into Blackjack. It is truly stimulating.

Of course the more hands the game consists of, the more the player's tactical acumen becomes important; for example if there are only two players, in just 10 hands the game is in favour of the person who is second in the last hand.

Concessionaires typically offer – again, similar to poker – both Sit&Go and scheduled tournaments. There is no starting time for Sit&Go games, but rather the tournament begins when the table has enough players. The scheduled tournaments on the other hand, have a set starting time, a maximum (normally high) number of players and are held at several tables. As the game progresses and players are eliminated, those still in the game are regrouped, thus reducing the number of tables until the final challenge. It is without a doubt the most interesting and exciting model.

THE LEGISLATIVE SITUATION

Developments in technology and especially the rise of the internet have rapidly changed the international situation for games of chance and, more generally, gambling. The first software for online casinos and secure financial transactions dates back to the mid-Nineties and since then the market has grown constantly and is destined to keep on growing. While some countries ban Internet gambling, most legislation struggles to keep up and varies widely from country to country.

Giovanni Carboni, an expert in gaming regulations, explains, "In the early 2000s small countries and areas took advantage of the introduction of particularly favourable authorisation systems for distance gambling, meaning zero tax, with had the economic objective of attracting users and developing the industry. Among the most significant on the European market were Malta, Gibraltar, Alderney (a Channel Island) and the Isle of Man, but some of the so-called dot-com poker operators even used licenses issued by the Authority of Kahnawake, an Indian reserve in Quebec. However, the game offered by dot-com sites was illegal in almost all European countries. In Italy it is a crime not only to provide and promote the game, but also to play on dot-com sites. In Europe only the United Kingdom permits cross-border gaming. Other countries tolerated it while the phenomenon of online gambling was in early days, once it became socially and economically relevant they banned and sanctioned it. In terms of the UK stance, it must be remembered that Gibraltar is an overseas territory of the United Kingdom, Alderney and the Isle of Man are Crown Dependencies of the United Kingdom and Malta gained independence from Britain in 1964. The European Community has recognised that the gambling sector is unique and that a national concessionary regime that imposes limitations on the circulation of services is acceptable, as long as it aims for public order and protection from criminal activity and is not discriminatory. The Italian system is an example of one of these and in fact many foreign service providers have entered our market. Other European countries, including France and Spain, are keen observers of our model, as increasingly more of them are updating their own online gaming regulations."